The Crusades

from Medieval European and Muslim Perspectives

A Unit of Study for Grades 7-12

by
Kamran Scot Aghaie

COUNCIL ON ISLAMIC EDUCATION

and

NATIONAL CENTER FOR HISTORY IN THE SCHOOLS
University of California, Los Angeles

Acknowledgments

This new teaching unit has been developed collaboratively by the Council on Islamic Education (CIE) and the National Center for History in the Schools (NCHS). Gary B. Nash, Director of NCHS and Shabbir Mansuri, Founding Director of CIE, led this collaboration. Ross Dunn, Director of NCHS World History Projects, made editorial contributions and helped facilitate the organizations' working relationship. Munir A. Shaikh oversaw the development and desktop publishing of this unit.

For information on additional teaching units and other resources produced by NCHS and CIE collaboratively or independently, write, fax or email:

Council on Islamic Education

Office Address:
9300 Gardenia Street #B-3 Fountain Valley, CA 92708
Mailing Address:
P.O. Box 20186   Fountain Valley, CA 92728-0186
tel: 714-839-2929 • fax: 714-839-2714
e-mail: info@cie.org
website: http://www.cie.org/

National Center for History in the Schools

University of California, Los Angeles
5262 Bunche Hall
405 Hilgard Avenue
Los Angeles, California 90095-1473
fax: 310-267-2103
website: http://www.sscnet.ucla.edu/nchs/

The Crusades from Medieval European and Muslim Perspectives

TABLE OF CONTENTS

Teacher's Guide

Approach and Rationale

In 1997, the Council on Islamic Education (CIE) began coproducing teaching units with the National Center for History in the Schools (NCHS). By collaborating on an organizational level, CIE and NCHS are able to benefit from each organization's respective strengths and reinforce the goal of producing much-needed resources for teachers. In order to broaden the scope of students' historical understanding, CIE and NCHS share the aspiration of addressing traditional topics from new or multiple perspectives as well as addressing underrepresented topics whose exploration helps complete the tapestry of history.

To this end, CIE has developed the following teaching unit titled *The Crusades from Medieval European and Muslim Perspectives.* This adds to nearly 50 teaching units available from NCHS that are the fruit of collaborations between history professors and experienced teachers of both United States and World History. They represent specific dramatic episodes in history from which you and your students can pause to delve into the deeper meanings of selected landmark events and explore their wider context in the great historical narrative.

By studying a crucial episode in history, the student becomes aware that choices had to be made by real human beings, that those decisions were the result of specific factors, and that they set in motion a series of historical consequences. We have selected dramatic moments that best bring alive that decision-making process. We hope that through this approach, your students will realize that history is an ongoing, open-ended process, and that the decisions they make today create the conditions of tomorrow's history.

Teaching units produced by CIE and NCHS are based on **primary sources**, taken from documents, artifacts, journals, diaries, newspapers and literature from the period under study. As you know, a primary source is a **firsthand** account of any event in history. What we hope to achieve using primary source documents in these lessons is to remove the distance that students feel from historical events and to connect them more intimately with the past. In this way we hope to recreate for your students a sense of "being there," a sense of seeing history through the eyes of the very people who were making decisions. This will help your students develop historical empathy, to realize that history is not an impersonal process divorced from real people like themselves. At the same time, by analyzing primary sources, students will actually practice the historian's craft, discovering for themselves how to analyze evidence, establish a valid interpretation and construct a coherent narrative in which all the relevant factors play a part.

Content and Organization

Within this unit, you will find: 1) **Teacher Background Materials** and 2) **Lesson Plans with Student Resources.** This unit is designed as a supplement to your customary course materials. We have chosen to pitch the various lessons on different grade levels, and they can usually be adapted to a slightly higher or lower level.

The **Teacher Background** section should provide you with a good overview of the entire unit and with the historical information and context necessary to link the specific **Dramatic Moment** to the larger historical narrative. You may consult it for your own use, and you may choose to share it with students if they are of a sufficient grade level to understand the materials.

The **Lesson Plans** include a variety of ideas and approaches for the teacher which can be elaborated upon or cut as you see the need. These lesson plans contain student resources that accompany each lesson. These resources consist of primary source documents, handouts, and student background materials, and in many cases, a bibliography.

In our series of teaching units, each collection can be taught in several ways. You can teach all of the lessons offered on any given topic, or you can select and adapt the ones that best support your particular course needs. We have not attempted to be comprehensive or prescriptive in our offerings, but rather to give you an array of enticing possibilities for in-depth study, at varying grade levels. We hope that you will find the lesson plans exciting and stimulating for your classes. We also hope that your students will never again see history as a boring sweep of inevitable facts and meaningless dates but rather as an endless treasure of real life stories and an exercise in analysis and reconstruction.

I. Unit Overview and Rationale

The purpose of this unit is to supplement the information presented in world history textbooks. While the Crusades are covered in nearly every world history textbook, the depth and breadth of coverage varies substantially. Furthermore, the Crusades are usually taught as a component of medieval European history without allowing for a more holistic approach, which would include various other perspectives on the Crusades. This unit provides students with primary documents that will allow them to practice their analytical skills by scrutinizing the uninterpreted texts on their own. This unit also provides new perspectives on the Crusades by focusing upon the experiences of both Crusaders and Muslims. Instead of looking at half of the picture, this approach allows students to better understand how two communities interacted with one another. And finally, this unit provides students with an understanding of the more diverse forms of interaction between Crusaders and Muslims. Students are exposed to examples of cultural, religious, military and ideological interactions that will allow them to assess the long term impacts of this encounter. Without implying that the military aspects of the encounter were insignificant, students can better appreciate the complexity of this important encounter between European Crusaders and Muslims.

The unit consists of five lessons. The first introduces students to the process of cultural integration and assimilation Crusaders underwent upon arriving in the eastern Mediterranean, an area often called the Levant. This lesson is intended to expose students to non-military aspects of the interaction between European Crusaders and Muslims. The second lesson provides students with a sense of the military conflict, including technological and strategic issues, as well as the military ethos and perceptions of their enemies. Lesson three focuses on Salah al-Din as an idealized Muslim leader and hero during the Crusades. Students will see how Muslims and Christian Europeans viewed Salah al-Din. Lesson four focuses on the emotional and ideological components of the interaction by providing students with direct evidence regarding the self-perceptions of the Crusaders and Muslims. More specifically, students will learn what individuals on both sides claimed were motivating factors in embarking on, or fighting against, the Crusades. The final lesson provides students with a variety of information about the experiences of women. While the study of the experiences of women during the Crusades is just beginning, it is possible to provide a general sense of how these women dealt with the situations in which they found themselves.

II. Unit Context

This unit is meant for use primarily in world history courses, or in courses that include material relevant to the Middle East or the Muslim world. Since it is assumed that students have covered basic World history beforehand, or are in the process of doing so, this unit must be situated within the general framework of Medieval European history during the time of the Crusades as well as Muslim and Middle Eastern history in order for students to understand the information given to them. Students must have already covered Islam and at least the rudimentary historical information about the Middle East and/or Muslim regions of the world. They also need to have covered developments in Europe in the ninth and tenth centuries which influenced the advent of the Crusades.

III. Correlation to National Standards for World History

The Crusades from Medieval European and Muslim Perspectives provides teaching materials to support the *National Standards for World History* (National Center for History in the Schools, 1996). Lessons within this unit assist students in attaining the following Standards:

ERA 5: Intensified Hemispheric Interactions, 1000–1500 CE

1C: THE STUDENT UNDERSTANDS HOW PASTORAL MIGRATIONS AND RELIGIOUS REFORM MOVEMENTS BETWEEN THE 11TH AND 13TH CENTURIES CONTRIBUTED TO THE RISE OF NEW STATES AND THE EXPANSION OF ISLAM.

Therefore, the student is able to:

7-12   Analyze how the migrations of Turkic peoples from Turkestan into Southwest Asia and India in the 11th and 12th centuries contributed to Islamic expansion and the retreat of Byzantium and Greek Christian civilization. [Analyze cause-and-effect relationships]

2B: THE STUDENT UNDERSTANDS THE EXPANSION OF CHRISTIAN EUROPE AFTER 1000 CE.

Therefore, the student is able to:

5-12   Analyze the causes and consequences of the European Crusades against Syria and Palestine. [Analyze cause-and-effect relationships]

7: THE STUDENT UNDERSTANDS MAJOR GLOBAL TRENDS FROM 1000 TO 1500 CE.

Therefore, the student is able to:

7-12   Analyze ways in which encounters, both hostile and peaceful, between Muslims and Christians in the Mediterranean region affected political, economic, and cultural life in Europe, North Africa, and Southwest Asia. [Analyze cause-and-effect relationships]

IV. Unit Objectives

1. To provide primary documentation of diverse Christian and Muslim experiences of the events associated with the Crusades.

2. To teach students about the military ethos, weapons, technology and strategies used by the Crusaders and Muslims.

3. To provide a holistic approach to the Crusades while balancing the focus between military and violent conflicts and social, economic and political interaction.

4. To provide depth to themes covered in K-12 textbooks such as ways in which Muslim and Christian cultures interacted and influenced each other.

5. Demonstrate the self-proclaimed motivations of both sides of the conflict in order to expose students to an uninterpreted perspective.

6. Provide information concerning the Crusader states and Christian settlements in the Middle East during the period.

V. Introduction to *The Crusades from Medieval European and Muslim Perspectives*

The Crusades is one of the most important subjects to be covered in world histor, courses, not only because of its relative importance to both Europe and the Middle East, but also because of its importance as a case study in cross-cultural interaction. While the Crusades were instigated by the call for holy war against Muslims by Pope Urban II in 1095, the outcomes of this movement, which spanned several centuries, had implications beyond the military encounter of two political entities. During the Crusades, Northern and Western European Christians came into direct contact with Muslims in the Middle East. This was a particularly significant occurrence in that these European Christians had little experience dealing with religious diversity and even less experience living as religious and ethnic minorities themselves.

The reason for this is that the Middle East has always been a religiously diverse area, while Europe during the medieval era was relatively homogeneous with respect to religion. The only significant religious minority groups in Europe were Jews, as well as a Muslim majority population in Spain, until the mid-13th century. The reconquest of Spain and the Spanish inquisition are good examples of medieval European Christian rulers' inability to find a constructive way to rule over a religiously diverse community. When the European Crusaders arrived in the Levant, they encountered a society where Christians, Jews and Muslims had been living in large numbers in the same communities for several centuries. While this society was not a multi-cultural utopia in accordance with modern sensibilities, it was a pluralistic society, with legal, political, religious, and cultural institutions that provided some semblance of peaceful coexistence for different religious groups, though relations were not always peaceful in practice.

An excellent example of the difference in pluralism between Easterners and European Christians, was the city of Jerusalem. The city had traditionally contained very large populations of Christians, Jews, and Muslims under Muslim rule, and at an earlier time, Eastern Christians presided over diverse Christian populations as well as Jews and others. The first act of the Crusaders when they conquered Jerusalem was to kill, deport or enslave the entire non-Christian population. This impractical and extreme policy, however, which was shocking to local populations accustomed to a more complex political order, was later abandoned by the Crusaders in favor of a system that was more practical and more in line with Eastern traditions.

The Crusaders arrived with the intention of fighting a holy war against people they thought of as pagans. They often ended up settling in the region, however, and adopting eastern Mediterranean ways of life to a considerable extent. The Latin kingdoms, the first of which were established in 1098, lasted for almost two centuries. Crusaders were thus exposed to political, economic and social institutions that were radically different from their own, which in turn had an impact upon the development of Western civilization. They encountered new technologies, scientific, philosophical and medical knowledge, legal institutions that allowed for religious diversity, luxurious commodities such as exotic clothing, spices and foods. They also encountered religious traditions with which they were unfamiliar. It is difficult to precisely gauge the extent of the Crusades' impact upon European culture, because interaction between Christian and Muslim societies took place in a number of arenas during that period, such as the Iberian Peninsula, Sicily and Italian merchant cities trading at southern and eastern Mediterranean ports. There is considerable evidence, however, that the Crusades provided many opportunities for interaction and fruitful exchange. In any case, Northern and Western Europeans who had little or no previous experience with Muslims came into direct contact at that time on many levels.

Between 1098 and 1109, the Frankish Crusaders carved out four settlements in the eastern Mediterranean: the County of Edessa, the principality of Antioch; the Kingdom of Jerusalem; and the County of Tripoli. In studying the Latin kingdoms in the Levant, several basic points should be kept in mind. The Crusaders were plagued by a constant shortage of manpower both in military and economic terms, which was a major consideration in almost all matters of state. This shortage led to the integration of Levantines into their political and social order. Crusaders also brought with them political and economic institutions which were, at least initially, ill-suited for the pluralistic environment in which they found themselves. This eventually forced them to make alliances with Eastern Christians and even Muslims (a practice which was not common in Northern and Western Europe at that time). The Crusaders made modifications to the feudal system as they had known it in Europe and incorporated other populations into their economic and political system. They also made frequent alliances with Muslims based on political pragmatism, on some occasions even to strengthen themselves in rivalries with other Frankish Crusaders. An excellent example of the Crusaders' adaptability was the adoption of the Muslim *jizyah*, which was a special tax paid by Christians and Jews under Muslim rule. The Crusaders simply reversed the process by having Muslims under their rule pay a similar tax.

The Crusaders were not accustomed to the desert, or steppe terrain where they often had to fight and live. Finding their Northern ways impractical or uncomfortable, they began to adopt a way of life that was better adapted to the climate and society of the region, including food, medical practices, modes of economic production, and political institutions. Their adoption of trade as a means of livelihood is an excellent example of this adaptability. In the Latin states, trade became a major source of economic benefit to the Frankish Crusaders, who began to serve as middle-men in the growing trade between East and West. These mostly Northern European settlers were relatively new to a trade-driven economic system, requiring them to adjust to an environment in which links with European trading cities like Venice and Genoa, as well as knowledge of conditions farther East were critically important to economic survival.

For most Muslims of the region, the advent of the Crusades was a fairly insignificant event that initially had little direct effect on their lives. The Crusaders had taken control of a relatively small area of land and did not pose a significant threat to the livelihood and existence of most Muslims. Furthermore, Muslims did not generally view this encounter as an epic conflict between a "Muslim East" and a "Christian West." This perception developed only gradually, and to a considerable extent in retrospect, as the conflict passed into legend and popular culture. At the time of the first Crusade in the late 11th century, the Muslim population in most parts of the Middle East was only slightly greater than 50 percent.[1] In almost every region of the Middle East there were very large Christian communities (such as Nestorians, Maronites, Assyrians, Armenians, Copts, Jacobites), in addition to a large Byzantine state in Asia Minor. Muslims were accustomed to living side by side with Christians, cooperating and at times fighting with them.

The advent of the Crusades was not viewed as an unprecedented event by Muslim rulers and common folk. A Jewish account of 11th century Egypt describes how Muslims usually confused the Crusaders with Byzantine troops and thought that the victory of the Crusaders would be short lived.[2] The Crusades were also a more or less minor consequence of the long process of decentralization taking place within the Seljuk political order. The Seljuks were the Turkish dynasty that was ruling much of the Middle East, under an Abbasid figurehead, on the eve of the Crusades. This political fragmentation, which began with the death of the Seljuk ruler Malik Shah in 1092, was characterized by the emergence of innumerable city states ruled by competing local rulers. This political fragmentation not only made it possible for the Crusaders to invade without encountering unified resistance, but also helps to explain the attitude Muslims held toward the Christian invaders.

By studying the experiences of the Crusaders and their Eastern Mediterranean Muslim and Christian counterparts , historians can learn a great deal about cultural interaction between European and Muslim cultures. Such analysis is important because the region now known as the Middle East has been a point of origin for many of the ideas and technologies that contributed to the growth and development of Europe, particularly during the period following the Crusades and leading up to the European Renaissance. Furthermore, the study of interactions is an excellent example of the integrated or thematic approach to teaching world history favored by most world historians today. Such studies provide an alternative to the traditional approach of dividing the world according to regional and cultural boundaries and studying each region in isolation from the others. Educators too are increasingly overcoming the limitations of this traditional by striving for more realistic and comprehensive approach to teaching world history.

VI.   Lesson Plans

Dramatic Moments

Lesson 1   Crusaders Living in Muslim Lands

Lesson 2   Crusader Meets Mujahid: The Military Encounter

Lesson 3   Salah al-Din (Saladin): An Ideal Muslim Leader

Lesson 4   Ideals and Motivations for the Crusades, and the Muslim Response

Lesson 5   Glimpses of Women's Experiences During the Crusades

VII. List of Key Terms

al-Aqsa Mosque   [al AK sah] The Masjid (Mosque) located in Jerusalem next to the Dome of the Rock.

Adhan   [ah THAN] Muslim call to prayer from the mosque. (for more information see Mu'adhin)

Allahu Akbar   [al LAAH hoo AK bar]An Arabic saying which means, "God is great." It is said in many different circumstances, including during Muslim prayer and in the adhan.

Armenian   One of the numerous Eastern Christian communities living mostly in the Middle East and Armenia.

Ascetics   *See* Sufi.

Assyrians   One of the numerous Eastern Christian communities living mostly in the Middle East.

Caliph   [KAY lif] *See* Khalifah.

Copts   One of the numerous Eastern Christian communities living mostly in Egypt.

Dome of the Rock   A monument in Jerusalem built by Umayyad ruler Abd al-Malik in 691 CE. It is an excellent example of a Muslim structure that combines the style of pre-Islamic Byzantine architecture with Islamic decorative motifs. It encloses a large rock from whence Muslims believe the Prophet Muhammad made his nocturnal journey to heaven in one night in 619 CE (called the *Mi'raj*).

Eastern Christians   Large Christian communities have always existed in regions outside of Europe, in particular in the Middle East as well as Northern and Eastern Africa. Examples of such groups are the Copts, Armenians, Nestorians, Assyrians, etc.

Franks   The term used by Muslims to refer to Christians from Northern and Western Europe. This term is used to differentiate these Christians from the numerous Christian groups indigenous to the Middle East, such as Greek Orthodox, Nestorians, Armenians, Assyrians and Copts.

Hajj   The pilgrimage (journey) to Makkah (Mecca in modern day Saudi Arabia) undertaken by Muslims in commemoration of the Abrahamic roots of Islam. The Hajj rites symbolically reenact the trials and sacrifices of the Prophet Abraham, his wife Hajar, and their son Isma'il over 4,000 years ago. Muslims must perform the Hajj at least once in their lives, provided their health and finances permit.

al-Haram al-Sharif   [al HA ram ash sha REEF] This refers to the area enclosing the Dome of the Rock and the al-Aqsa Masjid in Jerusalem.

Jacobites	One of many Eastern Christian communities living mostly in the Eastern Mediterranean].
Jizyah	[JIZ yah] A poll tax paid by Christians who lived under Muslim rule in exchange for legal status and protection under Islamic law.
Khalifah	[kah LEE fah] Also called a Caliph [kay lif]. This is the term used to refer to the primary Muslim ruler. This office does not clearly distinguish between religious and temporal authority as modern political theory does, although his status does not correspond to that of the Pope in Rome, for example, or the Patriarch of the Eastern Church. Instead, the Khalifah ruled in matters of state and religious affairs, but his authority is limited by Islamic law. At any given time there has usually been, at least in theory, only one Khalifah for the entire Muslim world. However, during much of Muslim history there have been several other types of rulers with such titles as Sultan, Wazir, Shah or Malik, who exercised temporal political authority while recognizing the religious legitimacy of the Khalifah. Thus, the Khalifah at times functioned only as the symbolic leader of the Muslim world while these other rulers actually held political power. It is also worth mentioning that the concept of Khalifah does not involve the concept of divine right, though Muslims acknowledge that the Creator is the source of temporal power.
Kurds	An ethnic group based in the mountains of northern Iraq, Eastern Turkey and parts of Iran. They were traditionally semi-nomadic and, like the Turks, were superb horsemen and were very effective in battle. Salah al-Din was a Kurd who led a united resistance against the Crusaders that resulted in the expulsion of the Crusaders from the Middle East.
Latin Kingdoms	The small kingdoms that were set up by the Crusaders in the Middle East beginning in 1098. The four Latin Kingdoms that were established in 1098 CE were the County of Edessa, the principality of Antioch, the Kingdom of Jerusalem, and the County of Tripoli.
Maronites	One of many Eastern Christian communities living mostly in Syria and other parts of the Levant.
Masjid	[MAS jid] An Islamic house of worship, often called by the French term *mosque*, which was a corruption of the Spanish version of the Arabic original. The Arabic term literally means, "place of prostration" [the movement in prayer called *sujud*, in which the worshipper kneels with forehead, palms and feet touching the ground].
Minbar	[min BAR] A chair placed in a *masjid* (mosque), from where a sermon is given. It is positioned with its back to the *Qiblah*, which marks the direction of prayer facing Makkah, so that the person seated in the chair is facing the worshippers. It can be a simple chair or a raised seat standing two or three yards in height. It has no religious significance and is not a sacred space or object.

Mu'adhin	[moo ADH dhin] A person who gives the Muslim call to prayer (called the Adhan). Historically, the call was made from the top of the minaret five times per day at the appointed prayer times. (In modern times, loudspeakers are often used instead) The adhan consists of a simple Arabic verse recited in a style that incorporates some musical elements.
Mujahid	[moo JAH hid] A person engaged in Jihad [jee HAAD]. Within the context of the Crusades, this term was used by Muslims to refer to warriors or soldiers who defended Muslim lands in the face of Crusader armies. The term literally means, a person who struggles in the path of God.
Nestorian	One of the numerous Eastern Christian communities living mostly in the Middle East, but also in Central Asia.
Occidental	Europeans, Westerners. It means the opposite of Oriental.
Old Men	Refers to Sufis or Islamic mystics.
Orientals	Peoples living East of Europe, including the Middle East, North Africa, and all parts of Asia. It is the opposite of Occidental.
Qadi	[KAH dee] A judge in an Islamic court, who gives rulings on religious and secular matters. These rulings were historically enforced by the authority of the state. Qadis usually received their education in law and religious sciences from a Madrasah, the primary Islamic institution of higher education since the 12th century.
Saracens	[SAH rah seens] The most common term used by Europeans to refer to their Muslim opponents. The term derives from an ancient Greek word designating Arabs.
Sufi	[SOO fee] A Muslim ascetic, or mystic, who believes that discipline, meditation, and denial of the material pleasures of the physical world are the only ways to spiritually experience God. The term Sufi may have originated from the practice of wearing simple woolen clothing or robes (the Arabic term for wool is "Suf").
Templars	One of the orders of knights that originated in the Middle East during the Crusades.
Turks	Term sometimes used by Europeans to refer to Muslims. The actual term Turk refers to groups of Central Asian nomads who came into the Middle East beginning as early as the 9th and 10th centuries. They accepted Islam and began a tradition of Turkish military rule that lasted into the twentieth century. The reason for the Turks' military success was their technological advantage with horsemanship and the composite bow. Their tribal organization was also highly effective as an organizational device in both war and politics.

| Zoroastrian | [zohr oh AS tri an] This religion, whose adherents lived mainly in the Iranian plateau, was established in ca. 1000 BCE. Zoroaster was the founder of this tradition and author of the Gathas. |

VIII. List of Key Names and Places

| Alice | (12th century) Melisende's sister who attempted to rule the principality of Antioch after the death of her husband in 1130. She encountered strong opposition from local magnates and attempted to find allies with other Crusaders, Muslims and Byzantine notables. However, she was eventually forced to concede power to Raymond of Poitiers. |

| Baghdad | [BAG dad] Established in 763 by the second Abbasid Caliph, al-Mansur who made it his capital. It reached its pinnacle of prosperity as a commercial center under Caliph Haroon al-Rashid in the 8th-9th centuries. This city, which is situated at the hub of one of the most fertile and economically important regions of the Middle East, was one of the greatest centers of learning and culture throughout the medieval period. |

| Cairo | This city, which is situated at the head of the Nile river near the highly fertile Nile Delta, was established by Arab Muslims who took control of Egypt in 641 CE. This is why they named it al-Qahira (Cairo) which means "The Victorious." Cairo has traditionally been one of the most important cities in the Middle East because of its very large population and its proximity to both the Mediterranean and the economically important and fertile agricultural lands of the Nile Delta, which were vital sources of food and tax revenue. |

| Damascus | This Syrian city has been known by its current name for at least 3500 years. In ancient times, it was ruled by Assyrians, Persians and later by Romans. The Arab Muslims captured it in 635 CE and it became the capital of the Umayyad empire. This city has also been a major center of learning and culture under Muslim rule. |

| Genoa | [JEN oh wuh] This Italian city was primarily known for its success in maritime trade in the Mediterranean sea. It was a major rival of Venice in the medieval period. Genoa's fortunes were already on the ascent before the Crusades, but their success in trade was greatly enhanced by the advent of the First Crusade in the 11th century. |

| al-Harawi | [al hah RAH wee] An 11th century Qadi (Muslim Judge) in Damascus. He is chiefly remembered for his appeal (in 1099 CE) to the Caliph in Baghdad to defend the Muslims from what he described as an assault on Islam by Christendom. |

Jerusalem	Jerusalem's history dates back to at least 1900 BCE when it was the capital of the Cannanite city state. At around 1220 BCE the Hebrews, led by Joshua, defeated the ruler of this city, and later king David (r. 1010-970 BCE) made it the capital of ancient Israel. His successor, King Solomon, built the first Temple in 952 BCE. The Babylonian ruler Nebuchednezar captured the city in 586 BCE, and later it was conquered by the Persians, the Parthians, the Romans, and eventually the Byzantines, who held the city until it was taken by Muslims under Caliph Umar in 736 CE. Following this event, the Muslim holy sites — the Dome of the Rock and Masjid al-Aqsa —were built. Earlier, under Byzantine rule, the city had become the site of a great deal of construction with the Church of the Holy Sepulchre being built on what Christians believed to be the site of Christ's crucifixion in Jerusalem. Jerusalem is considered to be a holy city by Muslims, Jews and Christians. It is the site of the ancient Jewish temple, as well as being the city in which Jesus is believed to have been crucified, and finally, it is the site where the Prophet Muhammad is believed to have departed on a miraculous nocturnal journey to the heavens in 619 CE. Jerusalem fell to the Crusaders in 1099 and was retaken by Salah al-Din's forces in 1187.
Knyvet, Alice	See Alice.
Levant	[luh VAHNT] The lands east of the Mediterranean sea stretching from the coastline all the way across modern day Syria, Lebanon, Jordan, Palestine and Israel.
Mas'ud (Emir)	[mas OOD] Father of Saljuqah and the Seljuk ruler of Anatolia and Syria. He held wide sway in this region and was responsible for conquering most of Anatolia from the Byzantines.
Mas'udi Princess	[mas OO dee] *See* Saljuqah.
Mecca/Makkah	An ancient city situated in what is today the state of Saudi Arabia. It is the birth place of the Prophet Muhammad. Muslims believe that this city is the site where Prophets Isma'il and Abraham built the Ka'bah as the first house of prayer dedicated to the worship of the One God. The Ka'bah, which is the most important structure in the city, is an empty cube-shaped structure that serves as the axis around which Muslims pray and make the pilgrimage known as the Hajj. The Ka'bah is made of stone and is covered by a black and gold cloth embroidered with verses from the Qur'an.
Melisende	(c. 1002-61 CE) Daughter of the famous Crusader king Baldwin II and Queen of Jerusalem. When her father died she and her husband Fulk V were crowned king and queen. She proved to be a capable ruler and continued to exercise direct authority, even after her husband's death, as co-ruler and regent for her son Baldwin III. She was exiled to Nablus in 1152 but continued to be an important political actor.

Pope Urban II	(Odo of Chatillon) Pope 1088-99 CE. He is chiefly remembered for his positive steps toward moral reform as well as his call for the First Crusade at Clermont (1095 CE). He was a powerful motivational speaker and was able to rouse the masses, especially his French countrymen, to attempt to capture Jerusalem, but he died before they achieved this objective.
Richard the Lionhearted	(*Coeur de Lion*) King of England 1189-99 CE. He inherited his lands from his father King Henry II in 1189, and began preparations for the Crusade. En route for the Crusade in 1190, he captured Messina and Cyprus. Later in that year, Richard's brilliant victory at Arsuf resulted in the Christian capture of Joppa. Richard was widely respected by rulers and soldiers as a heroic and chivalrous ruler. He has often been viewed as the the ideal of the Crusader king.
Saladin	*See* Salah al-Din.
Salah al-Din	[suh LAH ad DEEN] Sultan of Egypt and Syria (1175-93 CE). He assumed control of Cairo upon the death of his uncle Shirkuh in 1168 CE. He focused his primary efforts on building up the economic and military strength of Egypt as he expanded his sphere of political control to include most of Syria. He eventually defeated the Crusaders in 1187 CE at the battle of Hattin, after which he retook Jerusalem. In 1192 CE, his troops were defeated by king Richard's forces at the battle of Arsuf, but he successfully defended Jerusalem. Later that year Richard made peace with Salah al-Din, who died a year later. In romantic European accounts of the Crusades, he has been remembered in as a noble Muslim leader. He is fondly remembered by Muslims as one of the most just, wise and heroic leaders in Muslim history.
Saljuqah	[sal JOO kuh] Seljuk princess and the daughter of Emir Mas'ud, the Seljuk ruler, and wife of the ruler of Amid with his capital at Diyarbakr. When Salah al-Din captured Amid, he allowed her to retain her position in the city, giving her the keys to the city, and allowing her husband to rule at her side. Ibn Jubayr recorded her grand Hajj to Mecca.
Seljuks	[sel JOOKS] This Turkish dynasty came from the central Asian steppes, seized control of Anatolia and much of Syria and Iraq, and occupied Jerusalem in 1071 CE. One of their most memorable accomplishments was the defeat of the Byzantines at the battle of Manzikert, after which they captured Antioch in 1085 CE. This battle is considered to be one of the catalysts for the advent of the First Crusade, which began in 1095 CE.

Shajarat al-Durr	[shuh juh ruht ad DOUR] She was a former slave of Turkoman origin who rose to a position of rulership in Mamluk, Egypt. When Salih Ayyub, the Sultan of Egypt, died in 1250 CE while the absence of his regent at Damascus, left Egypt open to conquest by King Louis IX of France, she organized the defense of the Nile Delta at Damietta. She continued to rule in Salih's name by hiding his death. Once it became known that Salih was dead, she handed the reigns of power to her stepson Turan but continued to exercise power indirectly through him. The Caliph in Baghdad sent a representative named Aibek to replace Turan. S she ended up marrying Aibek and continued to exercise power through his authority for another seven years. She died in 1259.
Sham	The Arabic term used to refer to the regions surrounding Damascus. It is sometimes used as a synonym for Damascus or Syria.
Sitt al-Sham	[SITT ash SHAM] Literally, "the Lady of Syria." She was Salah al-Din's sister and has been described as "a powerful, intelligent woman, with strong opinions, generous, truthful and kind." Her home was a place of refuge for people in difficulty. She built a college and a large tomb to the north of Damascus and endowed both. Thirty of her closest relatives were rulers. She died in 1219 CE and is buried in the school she founded in Damascus. She was the princess who was traveling with a Hajj caravan through the area of modern day Jordan, when Reynard de Chatillon broke the terms of the peace treaty with Salah al-Din and attacked the caravan.
Syria	The lands east of the Mediterranean. This term is often used loosely to refer to a region encompassing the modern states of Syria, Lebanon and parts of Jordan, Palestine and Israel.
Urban II	*See* Pope Urban II.
Venice	A city in northeastern Italy, which was created in the 6th century as a refuge from the wars raging between the Ostrogoths and the Roman Imperial forces. In the 11th and 12th centuries, state directed shipbuilding and trade organization allowed Venice to become one of the most powerful trading cities in Europe. It served as a primary arena of exchange and trade between the East and the West. Venice and Genoa were rivals in this Maritime trade in the Mediterranean region.
Zengi/Zenji	The ruler of Mosul (1127-46 CE) whose influence reached across much of Syria and Iraq. He was able to mount a series of limited military strikes against the Crusaders, but unlike Salah al-Din, he was never able to mount a unified Muslim counterattack.

IX. Teacher Resources

TIMELINE FOR THE CRUSADES

330   The City of Constantinople is "Founded" by Emperor Constantine on the site of the city of Byzantium.

638   The Muslim Arabs, under the leadership of Caliph Umar, take control of the city of Jerusalem.

1070   Seljuk Turks take the city of Jerusalem.

1071   Battle of Manzikert. The Turks defeat the Byzantine Emperor Romanus IV and take control of Anatolia. This battle is seen by some historians as being an important catalyst of the European call for the First Crusade.

1081   Alexius Comnenus I becomes Emperor of the Byzantine empire, which is still based in Constantinople.

1088   The Christian Patriarch of Jerusalem sends a letter to the Pope detailing what he considers to be persecution of Christians by the Muslim Turks.

1095   Alexius Comnenus I appeals to the Pope for help. Pope Urban II calls the First Crusade.

1096   The First Crusade is launched.

1099   Jerusalem is captured by the Crusaders.

1100   Baldwin becomes the king of the Latin kingdom of Jerusalem.

1147   The Second Crusade, led by Conrad II and Louis VII.

1171   Salah al-Din takes control of Egypt: The beginning of the Ayyubid Dynasty.

1187   Salah al-Din defeats the Crusaders at the Battle of Hattin and later captures Jerusalem.

1189   The Third Crusade, led by Frederick Barbarossa and Richard the Lion Heart.

1193   The death of Salah al-Din.

1204   The Fourth Crusade, the Doge Dandolo of Venice leads the Crusaders to sack Constantinople.

1218   The Fifth Crusade.

1249   The Seventh Crusade.

1291   The last Crusader stronghold falls to the Mamluks.

MAP OF THE EASTERN MEDITERRANEAN COASTLINE (12ᵗʰ-CENTURY)

Dramatic Moments

Speech by Pope Urban II

In 1094 or 1095, Alexios I Komnenos, the Byzantine emperor, was sent to the pope, Urban II, to ask for aid from the west against the Seljuq Turks who had taken nearly all of Asia Minor from him. At the council of Clermont, Urban addressed a great crowd and urged all to go to the aid of the Greeks and to recover Palestine from the rule of the Muslims...

Most beloved brethren: Urged by necessity, I Urban, by the permission of God's chief bishop and prelate over the whole world, have come into these parts as an ambassador with a divine admonition to you, the servants of God. I hoped to find you as faithful and as zealous in the service of God as I had supposed you to be. But if there is in you any deformity or crookedness contrary to God's law, with divine help I will do my best to remove it. For God has put you as stewards over his family to minister to it. Happy indeed will you be if he finds you faithful in your stewardship...

For your brethren who live in the east are in urgent need of your help, and you must hasten to give them the aid, which has often been promised them. For, as most of you have heard the Turks and Arabs have attacked them and have conquered the territory of Romania [the Byzantine empire] as far west as the shore of the Mediterranean and the Hellespont, which is called the Arm of St. George. They have occupied more and more of the lands of those Christians, and have overcome them in seven battles. They have killed and captured many, and have destroyed the churches and devastated the empire. If you permit them to continue thus for awhile with impunity, the faithful of God will be much more widely attacked by them. On this account I, or rather the Lord, beseech you as Christ's heralds to publish this everywhere and to persuade all people of whatever rank foot-soldier and knights, poor and rich, to carry aid promptly to those Christians and to destroy that vile race from the lands of our friends. I say this to those who are present, it is meant also for those who are absent. Moreover, Christ commands it.

All who die by the way, whether by land or by sea, or in battle against the pagans, shall have immediate remission of sins. This I grant them through the power of God with which I am invested. O what disgrace if such a despised and base race, which worships demons, should conquer a people which has the faith of omnipotent God and is made glorious with the name of Christ.[3]

Speech given by al-Harawi in 1099 in Baghdad

Wearing no turban, his head shaved as a sign of mourning, the venerable *Qadi* (Muslim Chief Judge) Abu Sa'ad al-Harawi cried loudly into the spacious *Diwan* [audience hall] of the caliph al-Mustazhir Billah, a throng of companions, young and old, trailing in his wake. Noisily assenting to his every word, they, like him, offered the chilling spectacle of long beards and shaven heads. A few of the court dignitaries tried to calm him, but al-Harawi swept them aside with disdain, strode resolutely to the center of the hall, and then, with the searing eloquence of a seasoned preacher, al-Hawari proceeded to lecture to all those present, without regard to rank.

> *"How dare you slumber in the shade of complacent safety, leading lives as frivolous as garden flowers, while your brothers in Syria have no dwelling place save the saddles of camels and the bellies of the vultures? Blood has been spilled! Beautiful young girls have been shamed, and must now hide their sweet faces in their hands! Shall the valorous Arabs resign themselves to insult, and the valiant Persians accept dishonor?"*

"It was a speech that brought tears to many an eye and moved men's hearts," the Arab chroniclers later wrote. The entire audience broke out in wails and lamentations, but al-Harawi had not come to elicit sobs. "Men's meanest weapon," he shouted, "is to shed tears when rapiers stir the coals of war."

If he had made this difficult trip from Damascus to Baghdad, through three long summer weeks under the merciless sun of the Syrian desert, it was not to plead for pity but to alert Islam's highest authority about the calamity that had just befallen the faithful, and to urge them to intervene without delay and halt the bloodshed. "Never have the Muslims been so humiliated," al-Harawi repeated, "never have their lands been so savagely devastated." All the people traveling with him had fled from towns sacked by the invaders, among the people were a few survivors of Jerusalem. He had brought them along so that they could relate, in their own words, the tragedy they had suffered just one month earlier.

The Franks had taken the holy city on Friday...Two days later, when the killing stopped, not a single Muslim was left alive within the city walls...The fate of the Jews of Jerusalem was no less atrocious. During the first hours of battle, some participated in the defense of their quarter, situated on the northern edge of the city. But when, in that part of the city, the walls overhanging their homes collapsed and the blond knights began to pour through the streets, the Jews panicked. Re-enacting an immemorial rite, the entire community gathered in the main synagogue to pray. The Franks barricaded all the exits and stacked bundles of wood in a ring around the building. The temple was then put to the torch. Those who managed to escape were massacred in the neighboring alleyways. The rest were burned alive.[4]

Lesson I:
Crusaders Living in Muslim Lands

A.   Objectives

Students will:

→ assess the extent to which some Crusaders assimilated into Eastern society and culture.

→ identify specific examples of Muslim and Christian interaction on a religious level.

B.   Background Notes to the Teacher

The most important point to be stressed in this lesson is the fact that the Crusaders set up small states in the Levant, or Eastern Mediterranean coastal region of Syria and Palestine. Some of these kingdoms survived for well over a century. This raises the following question: To what extent can the descendants of the original Crusaders be considered European by culture? The Franks should not be treated as a single monolithic group of Europeans who set out as Crusaders; rather, they should be viewed as individuals on a spectrum. At one end were the newly arrived immigrants, or warriors of The Cross. At the other extreme were the Christian descendants of earlier Crusader immigrants who were born and raised in the Levant, and who knew very little about the land of their ancestors. It should also be pointed out that at times the line between European and Eastern Christians could also be blurred, leading to confusion if students are not made aware of the distinctions.

It is also important to emphasize that Muslims and Christians had lived side by side in Muslim society for centuries before the Crusades. This co-existence was based upon Islamic law and guidelines for mutual tolerance. It resulted in a fairly sophisticated mutual understanding of each group's religion and culture as well as the development of traditions governing coexistence and cooperation. Crusaders who came from Europe did not have the benefit of such a long term interactive relationship with non-Christians, since much of Europe was historically less religiously diverse than most Muslim regions of Africa and Asia. As a result of long term residence in the Levant, however, these Frankish Christians became more sophisticated in their understanding of Muslims and generally more tolerant of non-Christian and differing Eastern Christian practices.

The environment surrounding the Latin Kingdoms in the Levant was therefore one of cultural diversity and exchange. That is not to discount the importance of the military encounters, but rather to give a more balanced and accurate picture of this long period of interaction, which involved conflict and cooperation, giving and taking, religious tolerance and intolerance. Students should also be aware that most Arabic primary sources refer to the European Christian Crusaders as Franj, [the Arabic term for Franks]. They should not mistake "Franks" for French, or use the blanket term "Christian" to refer to these groups, since most of the Christians in the Eastern Mediterranean region were Armenian, Assyrian, Nestorian, Coptic, Greek, etc. and should not be confused with European, Roman Catholic Christians. The term Crusader is the primary term used here because it is the simplest and most accurate term, since it specifically refers to those "Frankish" Christians who came from Europe to the Levant with the intention of fighting holy wars.

C. Lesson Activities

1. Read **Student Resource A** and describe the two types of Crusading Europeans. Using the characteristics identified in these descriptions, have the students look for evidence of the various ways in which so-called "Orientalized" Crusaders had adapted their lifestyles to the environment in which they lived (i.e. food, dress, marriage, etc.). Students should explain how these two types of Crusaders might have differed in their view of Muslims from those who had not adapted to Eastern culture.

2. Read **Student Resources B-1** and **B-2** and list examples of tolerance and intolerance of the Christians towards Muslims and Muslims toward Christians. Explain why each group behaved differently toward people of the other faith.

3. This is a role playing activity. Group students into one or more pairs and have them pretend they are two cousins of common European descent. One was born and raised in the Levant, while the other has recently arrived from Paris. Have the newly arrived cousin display displeasure at the other's relatively more tolerant relationship with Muslims. With each student representing opposing views on the issue, have them debate the issue of whether or not this is a good thing. A few students could perform this activity in front of the class, several groups can work on their own simultaneously, or it could be done as a writing assignment.

D. Questions to Guide Discussions

1. How did newly arrived European Crusaders' cultural and religious outlook toward Muslims differ from that of Crusaders who had been living in the Levant for a long time?

2. What views of Christians did Muslims hold?

3. Did Muslims and Christians seem tolerant or intolerant of each other's religious practices?

4. Identify specific examples of tolerance and intolerance in the sources.

5. In what specific ways did Franks demonstrate their adaptation to or assimilation into the culture and society of the country in which they settled?

Background for Students

When the European Crusaders first arrived, most of them had never seen a Muslim before. As the Crusaders settled into life in the Levant, however, they had children, grandchildren and great grand children. Some Crusaders' former homes in Europe became a distant memory shared only with their grandparents and recent immigrants. For this reason, many of the Crusaders could more accurately be called Levantines of Western European descent. This is important, because the Christians in Europe had very little experience dealing with non-Christians, since Western Europe was almost exclusively Christian at the time.

The Crusaders who had settled gradually became more and more like their Eastern Christian co-religionists, not to mention other faith communities like Jews and Zoroastrians. For example, the Eastern Christians (i.e. the Armenians, Assyrians, Nestorians, Copts and Greek Orthodox Christians), who had lived side by side with Muslims for centuries, developed a fairly deep understanding of the religion and diverse cultures of their Muslim neighbors. Likewise, the Crusaders, who arrived in large numbers, at first had little or no understanding of Muslim religion and culture. They eventually developed a more sophisticated understanding of their Muslim neighbors.

Muslims and Crusaders were engaged in military conflict, but they also lived side by side. They experienced a great deal of cultural interaction. Muslims learned about European Christians, and European Christians learned about Muslims and Eastern Christians. This is why many recently arrived Crusaders demonstrated religious intolerance, and many Crusaders who had already been there for a long time showed tolerance toward those of other faiths. After a residence of some time, many Crusaders adopted Eastern dress, ate Eastern food, and interacted politically, socially and economically with non-Christians.

Student Resource A

Crusader Accounts of Crusaders

Two accounts by Fulcher of Chartres, a 12th-century inhabitant of Jerusalem

1. Those who were strangers are now natives, and he who was a sojourner now has become a resident.[5]

2. We who had been Occidentals have become Orientals; the man who had been a Roman or a Frank has here become a Galilean or a Palestinian; and the man who used to live in Reims or Chartres now finds himself a citizen of Tyre or Acre. We have already forgotten the places where we were born; already many of us know them not or at any rate no longer hear them spoken of. Some among us already possess in this country houses and servants which belong to them as a hereditary right. Another has married a wife who is not his compatriot—[but rather is] a Syrian or an Armenian woman perhaps, or even a Saracen who has received the grace of baptism....Why should anyone return to the West who has found an Orient like this?[6]

Muslim Accounts of Newly Arrived Crusaders

Two Accounts by Usama, a 12th-century Muslim Chronicler in Syria

1. Everyone who is a fresh immigrant from the Frankish lands is ruder in character than those who have been acclimatized and have held long associations with the Muslims.[7]

2. There are some Franks who have settled in our land and taken to living like Muslims. These are better than those who have just arrived from their homelands, but they are the exception, and cannot be taken as typical. I came across one of them once when...my friend [said to me]: "A Frankish friend has invited me to visit him; come with me so that you can see how they live." "I went with him," said my friend, "and we came to the house of one of the old knights who came with the first expedition. This man had retired from the army, and was living on the income of the property he owned in Antioch. He had a fine table brought out, spread with a splendid selection of appetizing food. He saw that I was not eating, and said: 'Don't worry, please; eat what you like, for I don't eat Frankish food. I have Egyptian cooks and eat only what they serve. No pig's flesh ever comes into my house! So I ate, although cautiously, and then we left. Another day, as I was passing through the market, a Frankish woman advanced on me, addressing me in her barbaric language with words I found incomprehensible. A crowd of Franks gathered round us and I gave myself up for lost, when suddenly this knight appeared, saw me and came up. 'what do you want with this man?' 'This man,' she said, 'killed my brother Urso.' This Urso was a knight from Apamea who was killed by a soldier from Hamat. The old man scolded the woman. 'This man is a merchant, a city man, not a fighter, and he lives nowhere near where your brother was killed.' Then he turned on the crowd, which melted away, and shook hands with me. Thus the fact that I ate at his table saved my life."[8]

Student Resource B-1

Religious Interactions: Tolerance and Intolerance

Shams al-Din, the chief Muslim Judge (Qadi) of Damascus in the 13ᵗʰ century: When the emperor, king of the Franks, came to Jerusalem, I remained with him, as al-Kamil had requested of me. I entered the Haram al-Sharif with him, where he toured the small mosques. Then we went to al-Aqsa mosque, whose architecture he admired, as well as the Dome of the Rock. He was fascinated by the beauty of the minbar, and climbed the stairs to the top. When he descended, he took me by the hand and led me back towards al-Aqsa. There he found a priest who, Bible in hand, was trying to enter the mosque. Furious, the emperor began to browbeat him. "What brings you to this place? By God, if one of you dares step in here again without permission, I will pluck out his eyes!" The priest departed trembling. That night, I asked the mu'adhins not to give the call to prayer, in order not to inconvenience the emperor. But when I saw him the next day, the emperor asked me, "Qadi, why didn't the mu'adhins give the call to prayer as usual?" I answered: "It is I who prevented them from doing so, out of respect for Your Majesty." "You should not have acted thus," the emperor said, "for if I spent this night in Jerusalem, it was above all to hear the mu'adhin's call in the night."[9]

Usama, a 12ᵗʰ century Muslim Chronicler in Syria: When I was visiting Jerusalem, I used to go to al-Aqsa mosque, where my Templar friends were staying. Along one side of the building was a small oratory in which the Franks had set up a church. The Templars placed this spot at my disposal so that I might say my daily prayers. One day I entered, said *Allahu akbar*, and was about to begin my prayer, when a man, a Frank, threw himself upon me, grabbed me, and turned me toward the east, saying, "Thus do we pray." The Templars rushed forward and led him away. I then set myself to prayer once more, but this same man, seizing upon a moment of inattention, threw himself upon me yet again, turned my face to the east, and repeated once more, "Thus do we pray." Once again the Templars intervened, led him away, and apologized to me, saying, "He is a foreigner. He has just arrived from the land of the Franks and he has never seen anyone pray without turning to face east." I answered that I had prayed enough and left, stunned by the behavior of this demon who had been so enraged at seeing me pray while facing the direction of Mecca.[10]

Student Resource B-2

Religious Interactions: Tolerance and Intolerance (continued)

Usama, a 12th century Muslim Chronicler in Syria: I paid a visit to the tomb of John the son of Zechariah—God's blessings on both of them!—in the village of Sebastian in the province of Nablus. After saying my prayers, I came out into the square that was bounded on one side by the Holy Precinct. I found a half-closed gate, opened it and entered a church. Inside were about ten old men, their bare heads as white as combed cotton. They were facing the east, and wore (embroidered) on their breasts staves ending in crossbars turned up like the rear of a saddle. They took their oath on this sign, and gave hospitality to those who needed it. The sight of their piety touched my heart, but at the same time it displeased and saddened me, for I had never seen such zeal and devotion among the Muslims. For some time I brooded on this experience, until one day, as Mu'in ad-Din and I were passing the Peacock House (Dar al-Tawawis), he said to me: "I want to dismount here and visit the Old Men (the ascetics)." "Certainly," I replied, and we dismounted and went into a long building set at an angle to the road. For the moment I thought there was no one there. Then I saw about a hundred prayer-mats, and on each a Sufi, his face expressing peaceful serenity, and his body humble devotion. This was a reassuring sight, and I gave thanks to Almighty God that there were among the Muslims men of even more zealous devotion than those Christian priests. Before this I had never seen Sufis in their monastery, and was ignorant of the way they lived.[11]

Lesson II:
Crusader Meets Mujahid
—The Military Encounter

A. Objectives

Students will:

➥ describe Crusaders' and Mujahids' (Muslim soldiers') views of themselves and their opponents.

➥ describe the characteristics of warfare and other aspects of military interaction between Crusaders and Mujahids.

➥ identify a variety of weapons and military tactics used by both sides.

➥ analyze Crusader and Muslim ideals of courage, skill and honor in battle.

B. Background Notes to the Teacher

While Crusaders and Muslims differed in religious belief, culture, and tactics, they often held in common a loosely defined conception of military honor or chivalry. While both sides rejected each other's religion, and were at times confused by their opponents' military strategies, they were equally often quite impressed with each other's military skills, courage, and sense of honor. For example, each side sometimes praised the other for incredible feats of courage, valor, skill, strength and honor.

It should also be pointed out that Crusaders and Muslim Mujahids not seldom fought on the same side in battle. It must be kept in mind that the Crusaders lived and fought in the Eastern Mediterranean for centuries. During this period, the Latin kingdoms were often rivals , just as many Muslim rulers were often rivals of other Muslims. Neither the Crusader states nor the Muslim states were completely united into a single political entity or front. Therefore, as Muslims fought against rival Muslim rulers and Crusaders fought against rival Crusader groups, they often found it advantageous to build alliances with their former opponents. There are many historical examples in which Muslims and Crusaders formed an alliance with one another and fought against an opposing army that was also made up of allied Muslims and Crusaders. As a result, the degree of interaction between these soldiers and their leaders was often quite extensive.

Crusaders and Muslims used substantially different weapons and military tactics, or they used similar weapons and tactics in a different manner. For example, Crusaders rarely used full plate armor of the type often associated with the traditional image of a Crusader, but they did wear various types of ring mail and chain mail armor which were heavier than the body armor worn by their Muslim counterparts. Their swords and lances were also heavier and stronger because they preferred hand-to-hand combat and the mounted charge of heavy cavalry. Thus, the Franks were less mobile but stronger, but their heavy armor could be a terrible burden when moving through the desert in summer. It also slowed them down at times when rapid mobility was crucial to success on the battlefield.

The Crusaders' Muslim opponents, on the other hand, relied heavily upon speed and mobility in their tactics. As a result, they used different, less burdensome weapons. For example, they wore much lighter armor than their European counterparts, and their swords and lances were designed to be easily used on horseback, often at full gallop. Their style of fighting was strongly influenced by Turkish traditions of warfare on horseback that originated in the Central Asian steppe. Their weapon of choice was always the a small, "composite" bow of laminated horn, wood and sinew. This bow was not only small and light, but two to three times more powerful than the larger, heavier bows commonly deployed by the Crusaders. Muslim armies preferred to move in rapid alternating waves of attack and retreat on horseback. They often wiped out the enemy , by releasing a rain of arrows from their bows while facing backwards on their horses, riding at top speed. Muslim soldiers generally employed a straight-on attack with swords and lances only as a last resort.

C. Lesson Activities

1. Read **Student Resources A-1** and **A-2** and a list the adjectives Muslim and Crusader soldiers used to describe their opponents. Be sure to differentiate between positive qualities and negative qualities.

2. Examine **Student Resources B-1** through **B-11**. List the types of weapons, mounts, clothing, machinery and armor in the images. Compare the Crusaders' weaponry with that of the Muslim soldiers. How do they differ, and what do these differences tell about overall military tactics, strategy, or style of warfare?

3. This activity can be conducted in class, as a homework activity, or as an extra credit project. After reading **Student Resources A-1** through **B-11**, examine **Student Resources C-1** and **C-2**. Separate students into groups. Each group will draw a map of a fictional battle field in which Crusaders and Muslims are fighting each other. It could be a city, castle, river, or valley. Have students tell the story of the battle to the class, explaining the weapons and tactics used. Assign an outcome to each group in advance (i.e. either the Muslims win or the Crusaders win, or it is a standoff). Have students explain the reasons for the success of the victors by referring to the weapons and tactics used by both sides.

D. Questions to Guide Discussions

1. What impressions did Muslim soldiers and Crusaders have of each other?

2. Why would soldiers praise their enemies?

3. What qualities of their enemies did these soldiers praise?

4. Consider why the soldiers were enemies at all if they respected each other so much.

5. Using examples of the terms each side used to praise each other, what qualities in their opponents did soldiers respect?

6. What types of weapons, armor and technology were used by each side?

7. What were the advantages and disadvantages of the different weapons and tactics used by each side?

Student Resource A-1

Muslims Praising Crusader Soldiers

A Turkish Chronicler: They are good corsairs; they are men; and as such they behave....Were they not Cross-Kissing Christians, and so much our enemies as they are, they would be very worthy of our esteem; nay the best of us would take pride in calling them brothers, and even in fighting under their command.[12]

Salah al-Din: Regard the Franks! Behold with what obstinacy they fight for their religion, while we, the Muslims, show no enthusiasm for waging holy war.[13]

Crusaders Praising Muslim Soldiers

Gesta Francorum, Account of a Christian Chronicler: Who is so wise that he can afford to decry the skill, the warlike gifts and the valor of the Turks? Indeed they claim that none but the Franks and themselves have the right to call themselves knights. Certainly if they kept the faith of Christ, they would have no equal in power, in courage and in the science of war.[14]

Excerpt from the Primary Latin Biography of King Richard: The Turkish warriors, hurriedly seizing their arms, came thronging up and flung themselves upon their assailants. The men-at-arms strove to get in; as the Turks [tried] to hurl them back. Rolled together in a confused mass, they fought at close quarters, hand against hand, and sword against sword....Never has there been such a people as these Turks for their prowess in war.[15]

Student Resource A-2

Usama, a 12ᵗʰ-century Muslim Chronicler in Syria: "Among the Franks...no quality is more highly esteemed in a man than military prowess. The knights have a monopoly of the positions of honor and importance among them, and no one else has any prestige in their eyes. They are the men who give counsel, pass judgment and command the armies. On one occasion I went to [court] with one of them about some herds that the Prince of Baniyas seized in a wood. This was at a time when there was a truce between us, and I was living in Damascus. I said to King Fulk, the son of Fulk: 'This man attacked and seized my herd. This is the season when the cows are in calf; their young died at birth, and he has returned the herd to me completely ruined.' The King turned to the six or seven of his knights and said: 'Come, give a judgment on this man's case.' They retired from the audience chamber and discussed the matter until they all agreed. Then they returned to the King's presence and said: 'We have decided that the Prince of Baniyas should indemnify this man for the cattle that he has ruined.' The King ordered that the indemnity should be paid, but such was the pressure put on me and the courtesy shown me that in the end I accepted four hundred dinars from the Prince. Once the knights have given their judgment neither the King nor any other commander can alter or annul it, so great an influence do their knights have in their society. On this occasion the King swore to me that he had been made very happy the day before.

When I asked him what had made him happy he said: "They told me that you were a great knight, but I did not believe that you would be chivalrous." "Your Majesty," I replied, "I am a knight of my own race and my people."[16]

Student Resource B-1

Miniature of Muslims in battle[17]

Student Resource B-2

Image of knights fighting[18]

Student Resource B-3

Muslim Trebuchet[19]

Student Resources B-4 and B-5

European Swords[20]

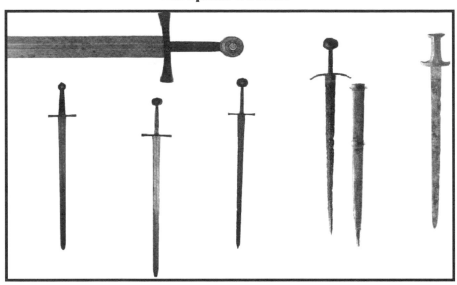

Muslim Swords[21]

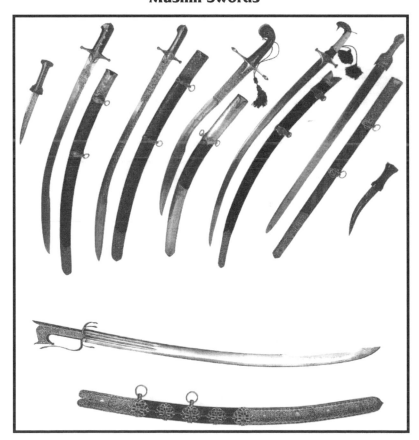

Student Resources B-6 and B-7

Composite Bow and Spearhead [22]

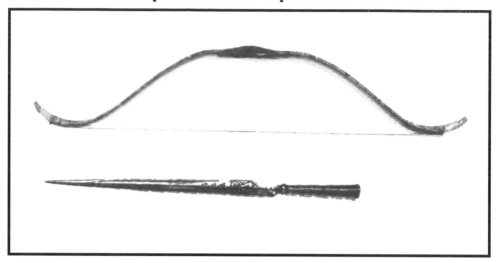

Muslims practicing with the composite bow [23]

Student Resource B-8

Muslims with swords riding in a circle[24]

Student Resource B-9

Muslim Riders and Ship[25]

Student Resources B-10 and B-11

Richard's Seal[26]

Templar Knight with a lance[27]

Student Resource C-1

Military Tactics

Baha al-Din, a 12ᵗʰ century Muslim Chronicler in Syria: A few of our warriors, mounted on good horses, advanced towards the enemy and discharged a flight of arrows at them, so as to entice them out into the plain; but they would not leave their camp.[28]

Baha al-Din, a 12ᵗʰ century Muslim Chronicler in Syria: The enemy had already formed in order of battle; the infantry, drawn up in front of the cavalry, stood firm as a wall, and every foot-soldier wore a vest of thick felt and coat of mail so dense and strong that our arrows made no impression on them. They shot at us with their great arbalists wounding the Muslim horses and their riders. I saw some (of the Frankish foot-soldiers) with from one to ten arrows sticking in them, and still advancing at their ordinary pace without leaving the ranks....Their troops continued to advance in the order we have just described, all the while maintaining a steady fight. The Muslims discharged arrows at them from all sides to annoy them, and force them to charge; but in this they were unsuccessful. These men exercised wonderful self-control; they went on their way without any hurry, whilst their ships followed their line of march along the coast, and in this manner they reached their halting place.[29]

Student Resource C-2

Technology (canons, gunpowder, bombs, etc.)

Baha al-Din, a 12th century Muslim Chronicler in Syria: ...the king of the Germans turned his attention to attacking the city, and took care that the blockade was maintained very strictly. He had some extraordinary engines made of a most peculiar construction, the terrible aspect of which made the garrison fear for the safety of the city. Among these new inventions was a great machine, covered with iron plates and mounted on wheels, that would accommodate a great number of soldiers. It was furnished with a huge head with a strong iron neck which was to butt against the walls. It was called a ram.[30]

The famous 13th-14th century chronicler Jean Sire de Joinville: One of the fighting officers at the battle recorded that when the French commander saw the 'Saracens' preparing to discharge the fire 'he announced in panic that they were irretrievably lost.' The fire was discharged, it is said, from a large *ballista* (giant crossbow) in Iraqi pots (*qidr 'Iraqi*)....De Joinville wrote, "It was like a big cask and had a tail the length of a large spear: The noise it made resembled thunder and it appeared like a great fiery dragon flying through the air, giving such a light that we could see in our camp as clearly as in broad daylight."[31]

Ibn Khaldun, a 14th century Muslim Historian in North Africa: [The Sultan] installed siege engines and gunpowder engines; which project small balls of iron. These balls are ejected from a chamber placed in front of a kindling fire of gunpowder; this happens by a strange property which attributes all actions to the power of the Creator.[32]

Ibn al-Khatib, a 14th century Muslim Historian in Spain: He bombarded the upper part of the strong tower with a heated ball using the great engine which functions by means of [a combustible substance]. This bombardment caused ruin like thunder and the besieged surrendered unconditionally.[33]

The famous 13th-14th century Chronicler Jean Sire de Joinville: During the siege, it was said that the Sultan's trebuchets and catapults flung their "pottery containers filled with an explosive mixture at the walls of the city or over them into the town."[34]

Lesson III:
Salah al-Din (Saladin)
—An Ideal Muslim Leader

A. Objectives

Students will:

↪ identify the Muslim hero named Salah al-Din and describe his personality and achievements.

↪ describe Muslim and Christian perceptions of Salah al-Din.

↪ analyze concepts of piety, courage, leadership, chivalry and honor and explain why they were shared by both Muslims and Christians.

B. Background Notes to the Teacher

One of the most famous figures in the Crusades was Salah al-Din, known as Saladin in the West. Although he became famous as the Muslim leader who finally defeated the Crusaders, he has been praised by accounts on both sides of the conflict for his chivalry, justice, wisdom, courage and compassion. Salah al-Din became a mythical figure in both Muslim and Christian culture, and many others as well . His name appears in countless fictional and historical accounts from India to England. In European accounts, which were produced from the medieval period through the twentieth century, he is sometimes characterized as a hero and at other times as the villain, but his character is nearly always idealized, stressing his wisdom, kindness, and chivalry. Many European accounts compare Salah al-Din to one of the most famous of European Crusading king, Richard the Lion Heart of England. The personalities of these two opposing leaders came to epitomize the two sides of the conflict so much that it was widely but falsely believed that Richard and Salah al-Din fought a duel or a joust. Some accounts even portray Salah al-Din as having been knighted by Crusaders.

In this section, students are introduced to Salah al-Din's significance as a hero and a symbol of the ideal Muslim leader, who ruled with justice and united the Muslims to defend the lands taken by the Crusaders. This attribution of wisdom, justice, kindness and chivalry as qualities reveals a great deal about the qualities Muslims of this period wished to see in their leaders. For example, he was not seen primarily as a warrior king but rather as a ruler in the broader sense, which includes many non-military qualities. The qualities for which he is praised revolve around Muslim ideals of justice, piety and good conduct rather than military courage or prowess alone. This contrasts with the greater emphasis placed upon military prowess by the Crusaders with regard to their rulers.

Students are often confused by the realization that Muslims did not immediately unite against the external threat posed by the European invaders. In order to explain why that is the case, it should be stressed that the Crusades came at a time when the eastern Mediterranean was immersed in a period of political fragmentation, with many different states competing for control of resources and territory. Furthermore, it must be explained that the Crusades were not generally viewed by Muslims as a major threat to their political or economic interests. The Crusaders controlled a relatively small area of land and Muslims were used to living side by side with Christians such as the Byzantines who formerly controlled those territories. Thus, many Muslims probably did not perceive the Crusaders as a major threat, nor would they have been aware of the European background and motives of the Crusaders, just as the Crusaders were not deeply acquainted with Islam and Muslim culture. The importance of Salah al-Din must be understood within this context. His historical importance is derived from his ability to put into motion a large unified military effort against the Crusades, and from the enormous cultural significance that the conflict has acquired in retrospect.

The importance of Salah al-Din, however, cannot be separated from his military achievements, namely the fact that he defeated the Crusaders and retook Jerusalem and other territories they had captured. In addition to unifying much of the Levant and Egypt under his rule, he was a sound administrator who mobilized Egypt's economic resources, which he used to support the large numbers of troops he rallied to the cause. His military project was the first truly large-scale military effort directed against the Crusaders.

C.   Lesson Activities

1.   Students should form groups and read **Student Resource A-2**. Have each group make a list of the terms used to describe Salah al-Din. As they present their list to the rest of the class, compile a master list on the board (one student could be assigned to do this, or a representative of each group could add the group's contributions to the list).

2.   Perform the same activity with **Student Resource B-2**.

3.   In a general class discussion, identify the similarities and differences between the two lists, marking items to identify both shared and contradictory items.

4.   Continue the discussion by showing students the two graphic representations of Salah al-Din in **Student Resources A-1** and **B-1**. Have students compare the Muslim painting of Salah al-Din with the later Christian European painting of Salah al-Din. Have them demonstrate how these graphic images represent the characteristics in both lists. They should try to explain how people graphically represent ideas, while they simultaneously compare and contrast European and Muslim perceptions of Salah al-Din.

5.   Using **Student Resources C-1** and **C-2**, have students compare perceptions of Richard and Salah al-Din by contrasting their respective images in **C-1**.

The Crusades from Medieval European and Muslim Perspectives

D. Questions to Guide Discussions

1. How do the graphic representations illustrate the character of Salah al-Din?

2. What do European and Muslim perceptions have in common? How do they differ?

3. Why do you think many European writers portrayed a duel between Richard and Salah al-Din when such a confrontation never took place?

4. How are Richard and Salah al-Din portrayed as being different, and how are they portrayed as being similar?

5. What do these sources reveal about Muslims' and Europeans' ideals of leadership? Can we construct a rough image of the ideals leader for each of these communities?

6. How useful are graphic representations as historical evidence? To what extent might they represent actual historical events, as opposed to merely representing historical perceptions and ideals?

7. What issues should be kept in mind when using graphic representations as historical sources?

Student Resource A-1

Muslim Representation of Salah al-Din[35]

Student Resource A-2

Ibn Jubayr, a 12ᵗʰ-century Muslim Chronicler: God in His mercy gave to the Muslims here this Sultan, who never retires to a place of rest, nor long abides at ease, nor ceases to make his saddle his council chamber.[36]

A Letter from Salah al-Din to His Son: My son, I commend you to the most high God, the fountain of all goodness. Do His will, for that way lies peace. Abstain from the shedding of blood; trust not to that, for blood that is spilled never slumbers. Seek to win the hearts of the people, and watch over their prosperity, for it is to secure their happiness that you are appointed by God and by me. I have become great as I am because I have won men's hearts by gentleness and kindness.[37]

A Prayer Offered by a Muslim to God in Response to Salah al-Din's Recapture of Jerusalem: And prolong, O Almighty God, the reign of thy servant, humbly reverent, for thy favor thankful, grateful for thy gifts, thy sharp sword and shining torch, the champion of thy faith and defender of thy Holy Land, the firmly resisting, the great al-Malik al-Nasir [Salah al-Din], the unifier of the true religion, the vanquisher of the worshipper of the Cross, Salah al-Dunya wa al-Din. Saladin, Sultan of Islam and of the Muslims, purifier of the holy temple, Abu al-Muzaffar Yusuf, son of Ayyub, reviver of the empire of the Commander of the Faithful. Grant, O God, that his empire may surround his standards, preserve him for the good of Islam; protect him for the profit of the faith; and extend his dominion over the regions of the East and of the West.[38]

Baha al-Din, a 12ᵗʰ-century Muslim Chronicler in Syria: ...in the midst of our campaign against the Franks, Salah al-Din summoned his close companions. In his hand was a letter he had just finished reading, and when he tried to speak, he broke down. Seeing him in this state, we were unable to hold back our own tears, even though we did not know what was the matter. Finally, his voice choked with tears, he said, "Taqi al-Din, my nephew, is dead." Then his warm tears began to flow again, as did ours. When I regained my composure I said to him, "Let us not forget the campaign in which we are engaged, and let us ask God to forgive us for having abandoned ourselves to this grief." Salah al-Din agreed. "Yes," he said, "may God forgive me! May God forgive me!" He repeated these words several times, and then he added, "Let no one know what has happened!" Then he had rose water brought to wash his eyes.[39]

Baha al-Din, a 12th-century Muslim Chronicler in Syria: A few of our warriors, mounted on good horses, advanced towards the enemy and discharged a flight of arrows at them, so as to entice them out into the plain; but they would not leave their camp, having probably received information from some traitor of the real object of this maneuver. Nevertheless, this day did not pass without furnishing us with some cause of rejoicing; for forty-five Franks, who had been taken prisoner at Beirut, were brought in to the Sultan. On this occasion I witnessed the great tenderness of his heart, beyond anything ever seen. Amongst the prisoners was a very aged man who had lost all his teeth, and who could hardly move at all. The Sultan asked him through his interpreter why, being so old, he had come to this country, and how far off his home lay. He replied: "My home is several months' journey away; I only came to this country to make a pilgrimage to the Church of the Resurrection." The Sultan was so touched by this answer that he restored the old man to liberty, and supplied him with a horse to carry him to the enemy's camp. The Sultan's younger sons asked permission to kill these prisoners, which he forbade them to do. As they had made their request through me, I begged him to tell me the reason for his refusal, and he replied: "They shall not become accustomed in their youth to the shedding of blood and laugh at it, for they as yet know no difference between a Muslim and an infidel." Observe [Salah al-Din's] humanity, his wisdom and moderation! Al-Malik al-Adil, having given up all hope of enticing the enemy out into the plain, returned to the camp that same evening.[40]

Student Resource B-1

European Representation of Salah al-Din[41]

Student Resource B-2

European Christian representation of Salah al-Din

H.A.R. Gibb, a 20ᵗʰ-Century Western Scholar, eulogized Salah al-Din as follows: Neither a warrior nor governor by training of inclination, [it was Salah al-Din] who inspired and gathered round himself all the elements and forces making for the unity of Islam against the invaders [from Europe]. And this he did, not so much by the example of his personal courage and resolution—which were undeniable—as by his unselfishness, his humility and generosity, his moral vindication of Islam against both its enemies, internal and external, because they expected to find him animated by the same motives as they were, and playing the political game as they played it. Guileless himself, he never expected and seldom understood guile in others—a weakness of which his own family and others took advantage, but only (as a general rule) to come up at the end against his single-minded devotion, which nobody and nothing could bend, to the service of their ideals.[42]

Voltaire, an 18ᵗʰ-Century Western Philosopher: Salah al-Din never persecuted anyone for his religion: he was at the same time conqueror, humane, and a philosopher.[43]

Fictional Account Attributed to Salah al-Din's Uncle: I saw my nephew Saladin, who was King of Babylon and had thirty kings to govern under him, how he caused one of his retainers, a wise and prudent man, to mount and to ride abroad through all his good cities. And he bore three ells of cloth fastened to a lance, and he cried at every crossing of the streets: 'nothing more shall Saladin carry away with him [through death] of all his kingdom and of all his treasure, than these three ells of cloth for his winding sheet [funeral shroud].[44]

Fictional Account Regarding the Knighting of Salah al-Din (excerpted from the primary Latin Biography of King Richard): Hugh of Tiberias had been taken prisoner by Saladin (this actually happened in 1179), and before releasing him on promise of ransom, the Sultan took him aside, and begged him, by his faith towards God and his religion, to show him how knights were made....'I will not;' [said Hugh], and he explained that Saladin being void of baptism and Christianity, it was folly to talk of knighthood,...Saladin, however urged that he could not be blamed for doing it under compulsion, as a prisoner, and Hugh at length gave way. Then the ceremony began.[45]

A Christian Account of Salah al-Din's Justice: On the morrow the Turks came before Saladin, praying him on their knees for leave to avenge on these Christians the death of their fathers, brothers, sons and other relatives, who had been slain at Acre and elsewhere. To consult on this matter, Saladin called a council of his chiefs. Mestoc, Saphadin, Bedreddin and Dordernus were present and decided unanimously to give the Christians free passage and return. 'It would,' they said to Saladin, 'be highly detrimental to our honor, if by our duplicity, the treaty between thee and the king of England [Richard] should be broken. For thus would the Turks, which should be kept with nations of every creed, be reckoned worthless—and rightly so.' Accordingly, Saladin ordered his followers to see to the safety of the Christians both as they entered and as they left the city [of Jerusalem]. At his own request Saphadin was appointed to ensure the full observance of this injunction; and so, thanks to his care, in freedom and peace did the pilgrims visit the Lord's sepulchre—which they had so long desired to see. Whereupon, having met with the most generous treatment and finished their pilgrimage, they returned gladly to Acre....Now Saladin, as we have said, had set people to guard the roads when the pilgrims began their journey towards Jerusalem; and so thanks to this, we passed along without let or hindrance, and after crossing the mountains came to the Hill of Joy unharmed. From this spot we could see the city of Jerusalem afar off; wherefore, as is the wont of pilgrims, in great delight we fell down upon our knees and rendered humble thanks to God....Saladin allowed [the pilgrims] to kiss and worship the true Lord's Cross which formerly used to go to the war.[46]

Another Christian Tale: Saladin was most noble of heart and valiant and wise and generous. During a truce he once went to the enemy's camp to observe their customs. He admired the tables spread with white cloths, especially that of the King of France and his officers, who sat apart from the others. Then he saw how the poor ate vilely upon the ground, and he condemned the Christians for this—that they let the friends of their Lord eat below them, on the ground. In Saladin's camp they all ate inelegantly upon the ground, but Saladin had made his pavilion rich with curtains and carpets. The carpets on the ground were embroidered with crosses. When the Christians came to the camp they put their feet upon the crosses and spat upon them, whereupon Saladin said: "I see that you preach the cross and desecrate it like this. It seems that you worship God in words and not in deeds. Your manners do not please me, nor your conduct." He therefore broke the truce and continued the war which has not ended.[47]

Student Resource C-1

Richard and Salah al-Din in a Duel[48]

Student Resource C-2

Christian Account of Fictional Duel Between Richard and Salah al-Din (excerpted from the primary Latin Biography of King Richard): When he [King Richard] met Saladin in single combat *[which , as we know, he never did]* the Sultan was miserably discomfited. At the battle of Arsuf, for example, Richard did not miss the opportunity of personally worsting his "heathen" antagonist as well as routing his army....Saladin, in great dolor, fled to Cairo....He presently plucked up courage, however, to come back and challenge Richard in single combat...the event of the duel was never doubtful: no man could withstand Richard's arm.[49]

Excerpt from the Primary Latin Biography of King Richard: The Lord of the ages had given him [Richard] such generosity of soul and endued him with such virtues that he seemed rather to belong to earlier times than these....His was the valor of Hector, the magnanimity of Achilles; he was no whit inferior to Alexander, or less than Roland in manhood. Of a truth he easily surpassed the more praiseworthy characters of our time in many ways. His right hand, like that of a second Titus, scattered riches, and—a thing that is, as a rule, but very rarely found in so famous a knight—the tongue of a Nestor and the prudence of a Ulysses (as they well might) rightly rendered him better than other men in all kinds of business, whether eloquence or action was required. His military science did not slacken his inclination for vigorous action; nor did his readiness for action ever throw a doubt upon his military prudence. If any one chances to think him open to the charge of rashness, the answer is simple: for, in this respect, a mind that does not know how to acknowledge itself beaten, a mind impatient of injury, urged on by its inborn high-spirit to claim its lawful rights, may well claim excuse. Success made him all the better suited for accomplishing exploits, since fortune heaps spleen [tries with difficulties] on whomsoever she pleases, yet was not he to be drowned for all her adverse waves.[50]

Another Christian Comparison of Richard and Salah al-Din: The period [of the Crusades was such that] the warlike character of Richard I, wild and generous, a pattern of chivalry with all its extravagant virtues and its not less absurd errors, was opposed to that of Saladin, in which the Christian and English monarch showed all the cruelty and violence of an Eastern Sultan, and Saladin, on the other hand , displayed the deep policy of prudence of a European sovereign, whilst each contended which should excel the other in the knightly qualities of bravery and generosity.[51]

Comments of European Song-Writer, who composed songs about the Fictional Duel Between King Richard and Salah al-Din: When I began my plaint for the Lion, I found that I was in danger of defeat, for my rebellious brain could not give so many instances of his virtues as of his vices. But one does not lament the passing of a villain. Then there came into my head a certain strategy, which was to think that I was really making a song, for the great Saladin. So with the Saracen in mind—Saint Julian forgive me!—I composed a song for Christian Richard. Every good quality lacking in the Lion I discovered in the Sultan; the defects of the one were made up for by the other; and, believe me, I was so overcome by my own picturing of the glorious dead Sultan that I shed tears for scurvy Richard![52]

Excerpt from the Primary Latin Biography of King Richard: ...Saladin sent out a company to meet the bishop and conduct him with due honor to the Holy Places....He had the Holy Cross shown him and they sat together a long time in familiar conversation. On this occasion Saladin made inquiries as to the character and habits of the king of England [Richard]. He also asked what the Christians said about his Saracenes. To him the bishop made answer, 'as regards my Lord the king, I may say that there is no knight in the world who can be considered his peer in military matters, or his equal in valor and generosity. He is distinguished by the full possession of every good quality. But why waste words? In my opinion—putting aside your sins—if anyone could give your noble qualities to king Richard and his to you so that each of you might be endowed with the faculties of the other then the whole world could not furnish two such princes.' At last Saladin, having heard the bishop, patiently broke in: 'I know the great valor and the bravery of your king well enough; but, not to speak too severely, he often incurs unnecessary danger and is too prodigal of his life. Now I, for my part, however great a king I might be, would much rather be gifted with wealth (so long as it is alongside of wisdom and modesty) than with boldness and immodesty.[53]

Excerpt from the Primary Latin Biography of King Richard: The king [Richard] now sent word to Saladin and told him, in the hearing of his satraps [officers], that he only asked a truce for three years with the intention of going back home where he would collect money and troops with which to rescue Jerusalem from Saladin's sway. To Richard's envoys Saladin made answer that his regard for king Richard's valor and nobleness of character was so treat that he would rather lose the land to such a man, if lose it he must, than to any other prince he had ever seen...then when the truce had been reduced to writing and confirmed by oaths, the king departed to Caiphas, as best he could, in order that he might there be healed of his illness by medicine.[54]

Lesson IV:
Ideals and Motivations for the Crusades, and the Muslim Response

A. Objectives

Students will:

↪ identify the self-proclaimed motivations of Crusaders in invading the Middle East from primary source accounts.

↪ analyze primary source accounts to identify the self-proclaimed motives of Muslims in resisting the Crusaders' military advance.

↪ describe the importance of Jerusalem to both sides in the conflict.

B.   Background Notes to the Teacher

This lesson is designed to analyze the self-proclaimed motives of both the Crusaders and the Muslims. It is not designed as a complete analysis of the underlying economic, social and political factors that led to the Crusades. These lessons help students to understand the language and symbols that leaders used to motivate and mobilize their followers. While the Crusaders were probably motivated primarily by social and political changes happening in Europe, their own expressions of reasons for joining this religious and military endeavor are also important as historical evidence. On the other hand while the Muslim side was clearly defending against an invading force, it is important to analyze how Muslims themselves conceptualized the conflict through their own expressions.

Leaders among the Crusaders, as well as the Pope himself, put forth many reasons for embarking on the Crusades. They claimed that Muslims were killing Christians in battles with the Byzantine Empire and restricting Christian pilgrimage to the holy city of Jerusalem. More recent historical research has generally established that the problems of access to European pilgrims were due to unreliable security along pilgrimage routes through territory under Muslim rule. This was not so much deliberately caused by the Seljuk state, but more by its lack of control at certain times and places. At the same time, Christian pilgrim traffic to Jerusalem had been increasing due to Europeans' heightened interest and ability to travel. This raised expectations on the side of Western Christians and dramatized any hardships and disturbances to the traffic. The perception conveyed by the Church leadership, however, was that pilgrims were being interrupted or harassed due to intentional repression by Muslim or Turkish rulers. Therefore, the Crusades were usually portrayed as a mission in God's name against the infidels who must be expelled from the holy city of Jerusalem, killed, or converted to Christianity. Images of Islam and the Prophet of Islam were used to arouse anti-Muslim hatred. It is interesting to note that European Christian sources from the medieval period demonstrate gross unfamiliarity with Islam, its origins and religious practices. Some medieval writers falsely described "idols" of the Prophet Muhammad and "temples," where such worship took place, as well as distortion of other Islamic beliefs and practices.

As for the Muslim leaders, they stressed the idea of ending the Christian invasion of Muslim lands and the killing of Muslims. However, Christians were not viewed as outsiders by Muslims during this period, since Christians had been present in large numbers in the Middle East since long before the Crusades. In fact, Christians made up the majority in some regions. Like their Frankish opponents, however, Muslims in the region were most likely as unfamiliar with Roman Catholic doctrines and practices as their European opponents were regarding Islam. They viewed Franks (or Crusaders) as foreign invaders who had humiliated Muslims—and even affronted Islam itself—by taking Jerusalem, which is a holy city in Islam, especially because of the brutal way in which they did so. The Crusaders first massacred, then denied Muslims and Jews access to Jerusalem and turned the Dome of the Rock and al-Aqsa mosques into a royal residence. (On occasion they even prevented Eastern Christian rites from being observed in Jerusalem.) This made defense of Islam an issue in the conflict, and the Crusaders' acts gave the Muslims a compelling battle cry, as can be seen in al-Harawi's appeal at Baghdad.

C. Lesson Activities

1. Read **Student Resources B-1, B-2, C-1, C-2** and the **Dramatic Moment** accounts. Make a list of the reasons Crusaders stated as motivation to embark on the Crusades. Next, make a similar list of the Muslims' stated motivations in fighting the Crusaders. Compare these two lists.

2. Read **Student Resources A-1** and then break up into groups, with each group representing either the Muslims or the Crusaders. Have each group negotiate with another group representing the opposite side of the conflict. The main issue of the negotiations should be the status of Jerusalem. This negotiation should briefly outline the issues and concerns of the side it represents. As the starting point of the negotiations, each group should assume that the a military situation is a stalemate.

3. This is a role playing activity. After reading all of the Student Resources, have students work in groups during or outside of class. Members of each group will cooperate to portray a military leader leading his/her troops (please note that in rare cases women on both sides also organized and directed armies), with some representing a Muslim leader and others a Crusader leader. They will compose a short motivational speech to be given to their troops on the morning of the battle in which they represent the ideals and symbols for which these soldiers are likely to be fighting. Encourage students to be more creative than just composing a string of hateful comments about the enemy. Instead, they should give them positive reasons to give their lives in battle. These speeches can be written or dramatized orally.

D. Questions to Guide Discussions

1. How would you characterize the importance of Jerusalem to both Muslims and Crusaders during this period?

2. What concrete goals did the Crusaders describe as motivation to join in this military operation?

3. What concerns did Muslims express?

4. How do the excerpts describe Muslim and Christian views of dying while struggling in the path of God? How similar are these views?

5. How do the stated motives of the Muslims and Christians differ from one another? How are they similar?

Student Resource A-1

Jerusalem

William of Tyre's Account of the Crusader Conquest of Jerusalem: When they heard the name of Jerusalem called out, they began to weep and fell on their knees, giving thanks to Our Lord with many sighs for the great love which He had shown them in allowing them to reach the goal of their pilgrimage, the Holy City which He had loved so much that He wished there to save these good people. They ran forward until they had a clear view of all the towers and walls of the city. Then they raised their hands in prayers to Heaven and taking off their shoes, bowed to the ground and kissed the earth.[55]

King Richard's Message to Salah al-Din: Men of ours and of yours have died, the country is in ruins, and events have entirely escaped anyone's control. Do you not believe that it is enough? As far as we are concerned, there are only three subjects of discord: Jerusalem, the True Cross, and territory. As for Jerusalem, it is our place of worship and we will never agree to renounce it, even if we have to fight to the last man. As territory, all we want is that the land west of the Jordan be ceded to us. As for the Cross, for you it is merely a piece of wood, whereas for us its value is inestimable. Let the Sultan give it to us, and let us put an end to this exhausting struggle.[56]

Salah al-Din's Response to King Richard's Message: Jerusalem is holy to us as well as to you, and more so, seeing it is the scene of our Prophet's journey, and the place where our people must assemble at the Last Day. Think not that we shall go back therefrom, or that we can be compliant in this matter. And as for the land, it was ours to begin with, and you invaded it: nor had you taken it but for the feebleness of the Moslems who then had it; and so long as this war lasts God will not permit you to set up a stone in it. And as for the Cross, our holding it is a point of vantage, nor can we surrender it except for some benefit of Islam.[57]

Ibn al-Athir, a 12ᵗʰ-13ᵗʰ Century Historian in Syria: After the fall of Jerusalem, the Franks dressed in black, and they journeyed beyond the seas to seek aid and succor in all their lands, especially Rome the Great. To incite people to vengeance, they carried with them a painting of the Messiah, peace be upon him, bloodied by an Arab who was striking him. They would say: 'Look, here is the Messiah and here is Muhammad, the Prophet of the Muslims beating him to death!' The Franks were moved and gathered together, women included; those who could not come along would pay the expenses of those who went to fight in their place. One of the enemy prisoners told me that he was an only son and that his mother had sold her house to buy his equipment for him. The religious and psychological motivation of the Frank was so strong that they were prepared to surmount all difficulties to achieve their ends."[58]

Sibt Ibn al-Jawzi, a 13ᵗʰ-Century Muslim Chronicler in Damascus: As soon as the news that the holy city (Jerusalem) had been ceded to the Franks became known, the lands of Islam were swept by a veritable storm [of indignation]. Because of the gravity of the event, demonstrations of public mourning were organized....King al-Nasir asked me to assemble the people in the great mosque of Damascus, so that I could speak to them of what had happened in Jerusalem. I could not but accept, for my duty to the faith compelled me. [He said in the public event] "The new disaster that has befallen us has broken our hearts. Our pilgrims can no longer visit Jerusalem, the verses of the Qur'an will no longer be recited in its schools. How great is the shame of the Muslims today!"[59]

Student Resource B-1

Ideals of Crusaders

Slogan Used to Motivate Crusaders: Fight God's war and you will conquer, Fight the Lord's battle and you will be saved.[60]

Reflections of a Crusader Concerning the Sacredness of their Mission: Although nothing can resist the Almighty, he has decided to put to the test his followers in this world, even though he knows the fate to which they are eternally predestined. No mortal is allowed to scrutinize the secret of the divine judgment, but perhaps the merciful God, at a time when iniquity abounds and charity of the multitude grows cold, has wanted to offer the faithful a chance of safety, nay a cause of salvation, so that they who would give up all things for him will find him to be all things for all men." Christian account[61]

Comments by Pope Urban intended to Motivate Crusaders: Why fear death, when you rejoice in the peace of sleep, the pattern of death? It is surely insanity to endanger one's soul through lust for a short space of living. Wherefore rather, my dearest brothers, if it is necessary lay down your lives for your brothers, rid the sanctuary of God of unbelievers, expel the thieves and lead back the faithful. Let no loyalty to kinsfolk hold you back; man's loyalty lies in the first place to God. No love of your native soil should delay you, for in one sense the whole world is exile for the Christian, and in another the whole world is his country. So exile is our fatherland and our fatherland exile....."[62]

Bernard of Clairvaux of the Templar Order of Knights, Laying Down the Rules of Conduct for Templar Knights: The soldiers of Christ wage the battles of their Lord in safety. They fear not the sin of killing an enemy or the peril of their own death, inasmuch as death either inflicted or borne for Christ has no taint of crime and rather merits the greater glory....First of all, there is discipline and unqualified obedience. Everybody comes and goes according to the will of the commander. Everybody wears the dresses given to him, and no one goes in search for food or garments according to his whims. They live in a community, soberly and in joy, without wife or children....they cut their hair short because they know it is shameful for a man to wear it long. Never overdressed, they bathe rarely and are dirty and hirsute, tanned by the coat of mail and the sun.[63]

Student Resource B-2

Excerpt from a Medieval European Epic Poem: The emperor has captured Saragossa and has the town searched by a thousand of his Franks. In the synagogues and temples of Muhammad, with iron clubs and hand-axes, they smash Muhammad and all other idols so that no devilry or superstition will remain. The king [Charlemagne] is a true believer and would serve God. His bishops bless the waters and lead the pagans to the baptistery. If one of them opposes the will of Charles, then he has him imprisoned, burnt, or slain. More than a hundred thousand are thus baptized, made true Christians, excepting only the queen [Saragossa]: she is to be led captive to sweet France, for the king wishes her to be converted for love [willingly].[64]

Medieval European Song about the Crusades: God! We have for so long been brave in idleness! Now we shall see who will be truly brave; and we shall go to avenge the doleful shame at which every man ought to be downcast and sorrowful, for in our times the holy places have been lost, where God suffered death in anguish for us; if we now permit our mortal enemies to stay there, our lives will be shameful for evermore.

God is besieged in the land of his holy patrimony; now we shall see how those people will help him whom he freed from the dark prison when he died upon that cross which is now in the hands of the Turks. Know well, those who do not go are shamed unless poverty, old age, or sickness prevents them; but those who are healthy, young, and rich cannot remain behind without suffering shame.[65]

Speech by Pope Innocent: After you have led back Christians, you will convert the remainder of mankind, that is, Jews and pagans. The fish who live in the sea designate Christians for they are born of water and the spirit; the men who dwell on land signify Jews and pagans, they covet and cling to earthly things. But after all, Christians have returned to the obedience of the apostolic see, then shall the multitude of races enter the faith, and thus all Israel will be saved.[66]

Baha al-Din, a 12th-century Muslim Chronicler in Syria: ...the king of France had taken his departure for Tyre, and they had come to discuss the matter of prisoners, and to see the cross of the crucifixion, if it happened to be in the Muslim camp, or to know if it had been sent to Baghdad. It was shown to them, and when they saw it they displayed the most profound reference, prostrating themselves on the ground till their faces were covered with dust, and humiliating themselves in adoration.[67]

Student Resource C-1

Ideals of Muslims

A Poem by al-Abiwardi, an 11th-12th Century Muslim Poet in Iraq

We have mingled blood with flowing tears, and there is no room left in us for pity.

To shed tears is a man's worst weapon when the swords stir up the embers of war.

Sons of Islam, behind you are battles in which heads were rolled at your feet.

Dare you slumber in the blessed shade of safety, where life is as soft as an orchard flower?

How can the eye sleep between the lids at a time of disasters that would waken any sleeper?

While your Syrian brothers can only sleep on the backs of their chargers, or in vultures' bellies!

*Must the foreigners feed on our ignominy, while you trail behind you the train of a pleasant life,
    like men whose world is at peace?*

When blood has been spilt, when sweet girls must for shame hide their lovely faces in their hands!

*When the white swords' points are red with blood, and the iron of the brown lances is
    stained with gore!*

At the sound of sword hammering on lance young children's hair turns white.

This is war, and the man who shuns the whirlpool to save his life shall grind his teeth in penitence.

*This is war, and the infidel's sword is naked in his hand, ready to be sheathed again in men's necks
    and skulls.*

*This is war, and he who lies in the tomb at Medina seems to raise his voice
    and cry: 'O sons of Hashim!*

I see my people slow to raise the lance against the enemy: I see the Faith resting on feeble pillars.

*For fear of death the Muslims are evading the fire of battle, refusing to believe that death will
    surely strike them.'*

*Must the Arab champions then suffer with resignation, while the gallant Persians shut
    their eyes to their dishonor?*[68]

Ibn al-Qalanusi, a 12th-Century Muslim Chronicler in Damascus: The Franks cut the Turkish army to pieces. They killed, pillaged, and took many prisoners, who were sold into slavery.... When this event, so shameful to Islam, became known, there was real panic. Dread and anxiety swelled to enormous proportions.[69]

Comments of Ibn Ammar, 12th-Century Muslim Ruler of Tripoli: Every time the Franks took one fortress, they would attack another. Their power mounted relentlessly until they occupied all of Syria and exiled the Muslims of that country.[70]

Student Resource C-2

Ibn Jubayr, a 12th-century Muslim Chronicler: There is no excuse before God for a Muslim to remain in a city of unbelief, unless he be merely passing through. In the land of Islam he finds shelter from the discomforts and evils to which he is subjected in the countries of the Christians, as for example, when he hears disgusting words spoken about the Prophet [Muhammad], particularly by the most besotted, or finds it impossible to cleanse himself properly, or has to live among pigs and so many other illicit things. Beware! Beware of entering their lands! You must seek God's pardon and mercy for such an error. One of the horrors that strikes any inhabitant of the Christian countries is the spectacle of Muslim prisoners tottering in irons, condemned to hard labor and treated as slaves, as well as the sight of Muslim captives bearing iron chains round their legs. Hearts break at the sight of them, but they have no use for pity.[71]

Ibn al-Qalanusi, a 12th-Century Muslim Chronicler in Damascus: They [some Muslims] forced the preacher to descend from the pulpit, which they smashed. They then began to cry out, to bewail the evils that had befallen Islam because of the Franks, who were killing men and enslaving women and children. Since they were preventing the faithful from saying their prayers, the officials present made various promises, in the name of the sultan, in an effort to pacify them: armies would be sent to defend Islam against the Franks and all the infidels.[72]

Lesson V:
Glimpses of Women's Experiences During the Crusades

A. Objectives

Students will:

➡ identify various ways in which the lives of women on both sides were affected by the Crusades.

➡ identify elite women who participated in the Crusades and describe their involvement.

➡ compare and contrast the experiences of elite women with those of women from lower social and economic backgrounds.

B. Background Notes to the Teacher

Women's involvement in the Crusades, like other periods in the historical record, has not yet been properly documented. In order to avoid neglecting women's experiences entirely, however, this lesson presents some accounts of women's lives during the Crusades. It is important to note that the lives of women from the upper classes differed sharply from those of women from lower social and economic strata. Unfortunately, very little evidence about the lives of non-elite women has been discovered so far, and while it is certain that they were much affected by the Crusades, it is impossible to infer much about their lives from the stories told about elite women. These stories are very valuable, but they are probably not very representative of everyday life for the average women of that time.

There were substantial differences between the lives of Muslim women and Crusader women. Each lived under different marriage laws and traditions, different social customs and dress codes, and different views of femininity based on religious teachings. It is also notable that number of Crusader women in the Latin states was relatively small compared to the male Crusader population. This fact might have altered their status and roles in Crusader families and society relative to their status in European society. In any case, the lives of Muslim and Christian elite women probably had more in common than elite women of either group had in common with the lives of women from the lower strata of their own societies. It should also be kept in mind that elite women formed a very tiny minority in their society, whereas the vast majority of women lived in relatively impoverished conditions.

The lives of upper class women and lower class women differed in several ways. For example, both Muslim and Crusader women of the elite were less likely to become victims of war because they had access to the protection afforded by their status and wealth, such as body guards and servants. Elite women were valuable prisoners of war since they could be ransomed for a high price. Harming elite women could result in the loss of a great deal of money to the enemy. Ransoming of prisoners was a common practice during this period by Crusaders and Muslims.

Elite women also had greater access to political power, and they sometimes assumed leadership roles. They often exercised political power indirectly through their male relatives or directly, by using their titles, wealth, and personal authority. On the other hand, elite women were subjected to restrictions of various kinds. For example, modesty as a symbol of status for elite women, both Crusader and Muslim, was usually considered a very high priority by their families, which is why their access to the public markets, public baths, and other public spaces was often more restricted than would be the case with average women. After all, the average woman of the lower social strata usually had to appear in public in order to work, so their movement was less restricted than of elite women of either group. These non-elite women were also much more vulnerable to the ravages of war. They could find themselves bereft of their children or families, enslaved, or destitute if their husbands or other male relatives were killed or taken prisoner. While the story of women's lives during the Crusades cannot be completely told here, the sources allow us to catch glimpses of women's lives during this period.

C. Lesson Activities

1. After reading **Student Resources A-1** through **C-1**, compare and contrast the lives of elite women and average or poorer women. To stimulate discussion, create a list on the blackboard with two columns, showing the characteristics of elite women in one column, and the characteristics of average or poorer women in the other.

2. In groups, debate the following opposing positions: (a) Women were passive victims in the Crusades. (b) Women were active agents in the Crusades. Give numerous specific examples of women's participation in politics and war, either as passive victims or as active agents. Create a list of these examples from the sources, identifying each with Muslim or Christian society

3. Read all of the student resources for this lesson and form groups. Each group will select the excerpt that they believe best represents women's lives during the Crusades. The object is to analyze the nature and assess the usefulness of various types of historical sources. They should also assess the degree to which these women's experiences are representative of life during the Crusades. Students should consider the author of the source, the segments of society it represents, the type of source it is (e.g. a poem or historical narrative), and what types of questions can be answered by using it, and how useful it is as evidence. Each group will present their choice to the class and explain why they chose it.

4. As a group or individual project, write a short story portraying the hypothetical experience of a woman during the Crusades. Stories may simulate a primary source account, a literary recreation or contemporary interpretation. They may address the women's experiences specifically during the Crusades, but should include their experiences in general. These stories may be presented orally, followed by discussion of the status of women in these societies based on the student resources. Students may choose between these two topics or devise their own, based on the readings: (a) The story of a Muslim woman of elite status: the basic premise of the story is that a massive army of Crusaders have placed Jerusalem under siege. This elite woman becomes involved in a political negotiation in the absence of her brother who is the ruler of the city. (b) The story of a Muslim or Christian woman of common or lower class background: she has several children and her husband is killed while defending Jerusalem in the battle mentioned above. She and her children become refugees as they flee the city, and have nowhere to go.

5. Read **Student Resource C-2** and write a poem or song as a reading response, in groups or as an individual assignment. Students may choose to write a poem about a Muslim woman, or a Crusader's wife. The object of the poem is to respond to feelings of separation from a loved one, such as a father, husband, or sister, who has gone off to war or has been killed in war. Examples can be presented or displayed.

D.   Questions to Guide Discussions

1. What historical information can be extracted from the sources provided?

2. How did the lifestyles of elite women differ from those of the majority of women?

3. Were women primarily passive victims or active participants in the events associated with the Crusades?

4. Compare the lifestyles of elite Muslim women with the lifestyles of elite European Christian women.

5. Compare the lifestyles of average Muslim women with the lifestyles of average European Christian women during the Crusades.

6. Why do you think there are so few sources by, or about, women during the Crusades?

Student Resource A-1

Elite Women

Story Based on Primary Sources, Retold by Steven Runciman, a Modern Western Historian [the noble lady of Norman Sicily is the bride of the King of Jerusalem]: The [marriage] contract was made; and in the summer of 1113 the Countess set out from Sicily in such splendor as had not been seen on the Mediterranean since Cleopatra sailed for Cydnus to meet Mark Antony. She lay on a carpet of golden thread in her galley, whose prow was plated with silver and with gold. Two other triremes accompanied her, their prows equally ornate, bearing her military escort, prominent amongst whom were the Arab soldiers of her son's own bodyguard, their dark faces shining against the spotless white of their robes. Seven other ships followed in her wake, their holds laden with all her personal treasure. She landed at Acre in August. There King Baldwin met her, with all the pomp that his kingdom could provide. He and all his court were clad in costly silks; and their horses and mules were hung with purple and gold. Rich carpets were laid in the streets, and from the windows and balconies fluttered purple banners. The towns and villages along the road to Jerusalem bore like finery. All the country rejoiced, but not so much at the coming of its new, aging princess as at the wealth that she brought in her train.[73]

Ibn Jubayr, a 12th-century Muslim Chronicler: "The father of this woman is the Emir Mas'ud. His realm is large, and wide is his sway....This princess has provided many good works upon the pilgrimage road [to Makkah or Mecca], furnishing water-bearing beasts for this purpose, and a similar number for provisions. With her she brought around a hundred camels especially to bear clothing, provisions and other things."

[Saljuqah had held up the caravan for a day, by disappearing from her place.]

She [Saljuqah] returned at nightfall, and the arrows of conjecture flew at random concerning the cause of the departure of this much-indulged princess....One of the glories of this princess is that Salah al-Din conquered Amid, the city of her husband Nur al-Din, but left the city to her in honor of her father and gave her the keys. Because of this, her husband remained king. Saljuqah made a spectacular entry into the Prophet's mosque in Madinah. She was riding in her litter, surrounded by the litters of her ladies and her handmaidens and led by Qur'an readers, while pages and eunuch-slaves, bearing iron rods, moved around her, driving the people from her path....Wrapped in an ample cloak, she descended and advanced to salute the Prophet—may God bless and preserve him—her servants going before her and the officials of the mosque raising their voices in prayer for her and extolling her fame. She came to the small enclosure between the venerated tomb and the pulpit, and prayed there, wrapped in her cloak while the people who thronged around her were kept back by the rods.[74]

Ibn Jubayr, a 12th-century Muslim Chronicler: Salah al-Din's sister Sitt al-Sham was ...a powerful, intelligent woman, with strong opinions, generous, truthful and kind. Her home was a place of refuge for people in difficulty. She built a college and a tomb to the north of Damascus and endowed both. Thirty of her closest relatives were rulers. She died in 616/1219 and is buried in the school she founded in Damascus.[75]

Student Resource A-2

Elite Women (continued)

Ibn Jubayr, a 12ᵗʰ-century Muslim Chronicler: The Mas'udi princess entered at the head of her troops of handmaidens. The dome of her litter was wholly adorned with pieces of gold shaped like new moons, with dinars the size of the palm of the hand....The golden ornaments on the necks of her beasts and the mounts of her maidens formed together a sum of gold beyond estimation. It was indeed a sight that dazzled the eyes and provoked reflection....More than one of those persons worthy of belief, who knew the princess's affairs, told us that she is known for her piety and her charity and is celebrated for good deeds. Amongst these is her spending, while on the Hijaz road [to Makkah], a vast sum of money in alms and in generous payment of expenses of the road. She venerates holy men and women, visiting them in disguise from a wish to gain their prayers. Her conduct is remarkable, for all this is with her youthful age and immersion in the pleasures of the realm.[76]

Student Resource A-3

Miscellaneous Experiences of Women

Ibn Jubayr, a 12ᵗʰ-century Muslim Chronicler: We came across another striking example of [the state of Muslims living under Christian rule], such as breaks the spirit in pity and melts the heart in compassion: One of the notables of the town of Trapani [in Norman Sicily, which had previously been under Muslim rule] sent his son to one of our pilgrim companions, desiring of him that he would accept from him a daughter, a virgin who was nearing the age of puberty. Should he be pleased with her, he could marry her; if not, he could marry her to any one of his countrymen who liked her. She would go with them, content to leave her father and brothers, desiring only to escape from the temptation of apostasy and to live in the lands of the Muslims. Her father and her brothers were disposed to this proposal, since they themselves might escape to Muslim lands when the embargo that impeded them should be suspended....

We ourselves were filled with wonder at a situation which would lead a man to give up so readily this trust tied to his heart [i.e. his daughter], and to surrender her to one strange to her, to bear in patience the want of her, and to suffer longing for her and loneliness without her. We were likewise amazed at the girl—may God protect her—and at her willingness to leave her kin for her love of Islam....[77]

Baha al-Din, a 12ᵗʰ-century Muslim Chronicler in Syria: Once, when I was riding at the sultan's side against the Franks, an army scout came to us with a sobbing woman beating her chest. "She came from the Franks' camp," the scout explained, "and wants to see the master. We brought her here." Salah al-Din asked his interpreter to question her. She said: "Yesterday some Muslim thieves entered my tent and stole my little girl. I cried all night, and our commanders told me: the king of the Muslims is merciful; we will let you go to him and you can ask for your daughter back. Thus have I come, and I place all my hopes in you." Salah al-Din was touched, and tears came to his eyes. He sent someone to the slave market to look for the girl, and less than an hour later a horseman arrived bearing the child on his shoulders. As soon as she saw them, the girl's mother threw herself to the ground and smeared her face with sand. All those present wept with emotion. She looked heavenward and began to mutter incomprehensible words. Thus was her daughter returned to her, and she was escorted back to the camp of the Franks.[78]

Student Resource B-1

Women's Involvement in Politics and Warfare

Account of Usama, a 12th-century Muslim Chronicler in Syria: When the ruler of Damascus threatens to hand Damascus over to a conquering army in return for help eliminating his political rivals, the elites of the city call on his mother Safwat al-Mulk for help, "They therefore discussed the matter between themselves and represented the situation regarding the prince to his mother, the Khatun Safwat al-Mulk. She, in distress at this state of affairs and abhorrence of his action, summoned him and upbraided him in strong terms. Her benevolence, sound spirit of religion, and well-balanced intelligence moved her further to consider how this evil might be excised and the well-being of Damascus and its inhabitants restored. She therefore examined the position with a firm and prudent eye and sound judgment, and found no cure for the ill wrought by him save relief from him and the excision of the causes of the ever-augmenting disorder due to him. The leaders and chief officers of the guards advised her to this action, supported her judgment...[79]

Story Retold by Steven Runciman, a Modern Historian, Based on Muslim Chroniclers' Accounts: ...and Alice was left mistress of the city [Jerusalem]. But her position was precarious. Her main support came from the native Christian population. As her intrigues with Zengi [a Muslim leader] had shown, she had little regard for Frankish sentiment. She thought now of a better scheme. At the end of 1135 she sent an envoy to Constantinople to offer the hand of her daughter, the Princess Constance, to the emperor's younger son Manuel. Her action may have been, as the horrified Crusaders declared, due to the caprice of her ambition; but in fact it offered the best solution for the preservation of northern Syria. The Greek element was strong in Antioch. The Muslim menace was growing under Zengi, and the Empire was the only power strong enough to check it. A vassal-state ruled under imperial suzerainty first by the half-Armenian Alice and then jointly by a Byzantine prince and a Frankish princess, might well have served to weld Greek and Frank together for the defense of Christiandom. But the Frankish nobles were aghast, and the Patriarch Radulph saw himself displaced in favor of a hated Greek.[80]

Story Retold by Steven Runciman, a Modern Historian, Based on Muslim Chroniclers' Accounts: As she grew older, Queen Melisende took to pious works, though her chief foundation was intended for the greater glory of her family. She was devoted to her sisters. Alice became Princess of Antioch; Hodierna was now Countess of Tripoli; but for the youngest Joveta, who had spent a year of her childhood as a hostage with the Muslims, there was no suitable husband to be found. She had entered religion and became a nun at the Convent of St. Anne in Jerusalem. The Queen in 1143 bought the Church of the Holy Sepulchre, in exchange for estates near Hebron, the Village of Bethany; and there she built a convent in honor of Saint Lazarus and his sisters Martha and Mary, endowing it with Jericho and all its surrounding farms, and fortifying it with a tower.[81]

Student Resource B-2

Women's Involvement in Politics and Warfare (continued)

Account of Baha al-Din, a 12th century Muslim Chronicler in Syria: The Meeting broke up, and the subject of the peace was continually discussed. Messengers kept on passing to and fro until the preliminaries of the treaty were finally arranged. The principal condition was that the king should offer his sister in marriage to al-Malik al-Adil, [Salah al-Din's brother] on the condition that the pair should be put in possession of all the cities of the coast districts held by either Muslims or Christians; the latter were to be given to the princess in the name of her brother the king, the former to be granted to al-Adil in the Sultan's name. In his last message (to al-Adil), the king expressed himself as follows on this point: "All the Christians cry out against me for thinking of marrying my sister to a Muslim without having obtained permission from the Pope, who is the head of our religion. I am therefore sending an ambassador to him, and I shall have an answer in six months. If he gives his consent, the arrangement will be carried out; if not, I will give you my brother's daughter to wife, for which we should not require the Pope's permission."[82]

Story Retold by Charis Waddy, a Modern Historian, Based on Muslim Chroniclers' Accounts: Salih Ayyub's [the ruler of Egypt] wife was Shajarat al-Durr, who had been a slave of Turkoman origin. In 1249, The [Frankish] army of Louis IX of France landed at Damietta, at the mouth of the Nile River. Shajarat, acting as Salih's regent while he was away in Damascus, organized the defense of the realm. Soon after Salih Ayyub returned, he died. Shajarat concealed the fact of his death by saying he was "sick" and having a servant be seen taking food to his tent. She thus was able to continue to lead the army in his name. Turan, his son and her stepson, appeared and Shajarat handed the reigns of power over to him, finally announcing her husband's death. Still, Shajarat retained control, and rendered a crushing defeat on the Crusaders at Damietta. The leaders of the army did not respect Turan; they wanted Shajarat, seeing her as a Turk, like themselves. They plotted against Turan and had him murdered. On May 2, 1250, they put Shajarat al-Durr on the throne. As sultan, Shajarat al-Durr had coins struck in her name, and she was mentioned in the weekly prayers in Mosques. These two acts only could be done for the person who carried the title of Sultan. Peace was made with the Franks. Louis IX was ransomed and allowed to return home.[83]

Story Retold by Steven Runciman, a Modern Historian, Based on Muslim Chroniclers' Accounts: [The example of] Lady Alice Knyvet when faced with troops poised to take her castle probably reflects the motivations and actions of many who were forced into this militant role. "I will not leave possession of this castle to die therefore; and if you begin to break the peace or make war to get the place of me, I shall defend me. For [I would prefer to die] than to be slain when my husband comes home, for he charged me to keep it.[84]

Account of Baha al-Din, a 12th century Muslim Chronicler in Syria: Behind their [the Franks'] rampart was a [Frankish] woman, wrapped in a green melluta (a kind of cloak), who kept on shooting arrows from a wooden bow, with which she wounded several of our men.[85]

Student Resource C-2

European Women Left Behind by the Crusaders

A Letter from St. Bernard to the Pope Regarding Recruitment of Soldiers for the Crusade: You ordered; I obeyed; and the authority of him who gave the order has made my obedience fruitful. I opened my mouth; I spoke; and at once the Crusaders have multiplied to infinity. Villages and towns are now deserted. You will scarcely find one man for every seven women. Everywhere you see widows whose husbands are still alive.[86]

Medieval European Troubadour Marcabru: Her eyes welled up beside the fountain, and she sighed from the depths of her heart. "Jesus," she said, "King of the world, because of You my grief increases, I am undone by your humiliation, for the best men of this whole world are going off to serve you....Nothing matters now, for he has gone so far away."[87]

A Woman's Song by an Anonymous European Singer: Jerusalem, you do me a great wrong by taking from me that which I loved best. Know this to be true: I'll never love you, for this is the reason for my unhappiness....Fair, sweet lover, how will you endure your great ache for me out on the salty sea, when nothing that exists could ever tell the deep grief that has come into my heart? When I think of your gentle, sparkling face that I used to kiss and caress, it is a great miracle that I am not deranged....[88]

A Woman's Song by an Anonymous European Singer: I will sing to comfort my heart, for I do not want to die or to go mad because of my great loss, when I see that no one returns from that foreign land where the man is he who brings solace to my heart when I hear him spoken of, God, when they cry, 'Onward', give Your help to that pilgrim for whom my heart trembles; for the Saracens are wicked men.

I shall bear my loss until I have seen a year go by. He is on a pilgrimage; may God grant that he return from it! But, in spite of all my family, I do not intend to marry any other. Anyone who even speaks to me of it is a fool. God, when they cry, 'Onward', give Your help to that pilgrim for whom my heart trembles; for the Saracens are wicked men.

However, I am hopeful because I accepted his homage. And when the sweet wind blows which comes from that sweet country where the man is whom I desire, then I turn my face towards it gladly, and it seems to me then that I can feel him beneath my mantle of fur. God, when they cry, 'Onward', give Your help to that pilgrim for whom my heart trembles; for the Saracens are wicked men. I regret very much that I was not there to set him on the road. He sent me his shirt which he had worn, so that I might hold it in my arms. At night, when love for him torments me, I place it in bed beside me and hold it all night against my bare flesh to assuage my pains. God, when they cry, 'Onward', give Your help to that pilgrim for whom my heart trembles; for the Saracens are wicked men.[89]

A Crusader's Song (by an anonymous European singer): Oh, Love! How hard it will be for me to have to leave the best woman who was ever loved or served! May God in his kindness, lead me back to her as surely as I leave her in sorrow. Alas! What have I said? I am not really leaving her at all! If my body is going off to serve Our Lord, my heart remains entirely within her sway.[90]

Notes

1. Richard Bulliet, *Conversion to Islam in the Medieval Period* (Cambridge: Harvard University Press, 1979), 23.

2. Jonathan Riley-Smith, *The Oxford Illustrated History of the Crusades* (Oxford: Oxford University Press, 1995), 224.

3. http://www.fordham.edu/halsall/sbook1k.html

4. Amin Maalouf, *The Crusades Through Arab Eyes* (New York: Schocken Books, 1984), xiii-xiv.

5. Geoffrey Regan, *Saladin and the Fall of Jerusalem* (London: Croom Helm, 1987), 3-4.

6. Ibid., 2-3.

7. Ibid.

8. Francesco Gabrieli, *Arab Historians of the Crusades* (New York: Dorset Press, 1957), 78.

9. Maalouf, 229.

10. Ibid., 128-129.

11. Gabrieli, 84.

12. Ernle Bradford, *The Sword and the Scimitar: The Saga of the Crusades* (Milan, Italy: G.P. Putnam's Sons, 1974), 55.

13. Maalouf, 1.

14. Bradford, 54.

15. Based on the original chronicle *Itinerarium et Gesta Regis Ricardi* by an unknown 12th-century writer, reproduced in Bradford, 157.

16. Gabrieli, 73-74.

17. Michael D. Coe et. al., *Swords and Hilt Weapons* (New York: Barnes & Noble Books, 1993), 144.

18. Bradford, 102-103.

19. John R. Hayes, ed. *The Genius of Arab Civilization: Source of Renaissance* (London: Eurabia Publications Ltd., 1983), 212.

20. Coe, 39.

21. Coe, 141.

22. Ahmad Y. Al-Hassan and Donald R. Hill, *Islamic Technology: An Illustrated History* (Cambridge: Cambridge University Press, 1986), 98-99.

23. Bradford, 20.

24. Riley-Smith, 244.

25. Bradford, 205.

26. Stanley Lane-Poole, *Saladin and the Fall of the Kingdom of Jerusalem* (New York: G.P. Putnam's Sons, 1898), 299.

27. Riley-Smith, 196.

28. Baha al-Din, *The Life of Saladin* (London: Committee of the Palestine Exploration Fund, 1897), 239.

29. Ibid., 283.

30. Ibid., 214.

31. Al-Hassan and Hill, 111-112.

32. Ibid., 112-113.

33. Ibid., 114.

34. Ibid., 112.

35. Bradford, 136.

36. Charis Waddy, *Women in Muslim History* (London: Longman Press, 1980), 80.

37. M. Hilmy M. Ahmad, "Some Notes on Arabic Historiography During the Zengid and Ayyubid Periods (521/1127-648/1250)", in Bernard Lewis and P.M. Holt, eds. *Historians of the Middle East* (London: Oxford University Press, 1962), 81. Reproduced in Andrew S. Ehrenkreutz, *Saladin* (Albany: State University of New York Press, 1972), 3.

38. Regan, 154.

39. Maalouf, 178.

40. Baha al-Din, 239.

41. Charles Rosebault, *Saladin: Prince of Chivalry* (New York: Robert M. McBride & Company, 1930), facing title page.

42. Ehrenkreutz, 6.

43. David R. Blanks, *Images of the Other: Europe and the Muslim World Before 1700* (Cairo: Cairo University Press, 1997), 7.

44. *Récits d'un Ménestrel de Reims*, ch. 21, Stone Trans. p. 299. Reproduced in John Victor Tolan, *Medieval Christian Perceptions of Islam* (New York, Garland Publications, 1996), 29.

45. *Itinerarium Regis Ricardi,* reproduced in Lane-Poole, 389.

46. T. A. Archer, *English History by Contemporary Writers: The Crusade of Richard I, 1189-92* (New York: G.P. Putnam's Sons, The Knickerbocker Press, 1889), 327-329.

47. Gertrude Slaughter, *Saladin (1138-1193)* (New York: Exposition Press, 1955), 285-286.

48. Bradford, title page.

49. *Itinerarium Regis Ricardi,* reproduced in Lane-Poole, 378-379.

50. *Itinerarium Regis Ricardi*, reproduced in Archer, 6-7.

51. Rosebault, p. 261.

52. Slaughter, 288.

53. *Itinerarium Regis Ricardi,* reproduced in Archer, 330-331.

54. *Itinerarium Regis Ricardi,* reproduced in Archer, 315.

55. Bradford, 80.

56. Maalouf, 211.

57. Lane-Poole, 328.

58. Maalouf, 205.

59. Maalouf, 230.

60. Maya Shatzmiller, ed., *Crusaders and Muslims in Twelfth-Century Syria* (Leiden: E.J. Brill, 1993), 80.

61. Ibid., 75-76.

62. Bradford, 28-30.

63. Regan, 103.

64. *Chanson de Roland,* reproduced in Riley-Smith, 93.

65. *Canon of Béthune, 'Ahi, Amours! Com dure departie',* reproduced in Riley-Smith, 99.

66. Shatzmiller, 80.

67. Baha al-Din, 270-271.

68. Gabrieli, 12.

69. Maalouf, 17.

70. Ibid., 57.

71. Ibid., xv-xvi.

72. Ibid., 82.

73. Steven Runciman, *A History of the Crusades Vol. 2* (Cambridge: Cambridge University Press, 1962), 103.

74. Waddy, 84-86.

75. Ibid., 87-88.

76. Ibid., 86-87.

77. Ibid., 82.

78. Maalouf, 178-179.

79. George Richard Potter, tr., *The Autobiography of Ousama* (New York: Harcourt Brace and Company, 1929), 231.

80. Runciman, 198-99.

81. Ibid., 231.

82. Baha al-Din, 324-325.

83. http://www.fordham.edu/halsall/sbook1k.html

84. http://www.fordham.edu/halsall/sbook1k.html

85. Baha al-Din, 261.

86. Runciman, 254.

87. http://history.hanover.edu/medieval/crusades.html

88. http://www.fordham.edu/halsall/sbook1k.html

89. Riley-Smith, 103-4.

90. Ibid., 104.

Bibliography

Archer, T. A. *English History by Contemporary Writers: The Crusade of Richard I, 1189-92.* New York: G.P. Putnam's Sons, The Knickerbocker Press, 1889.

Blanks, David R. *Images of the Other: Europe and the Muslim World Before 1700.* Cairo: Cairo University Press, 1997.

Bradford, Ernle. *The Sword and the Scimitar: The Saga of the Crusades.* Milan, Italy: G.P. Putnam's Sons, 1974.

Ed-Din, Beha. *The Life of Saladin.* London: Committee of the Palestine Exploration Fund, 1897.

Ehrenkreutz, Andrew S. *Saladin.* Albany: State University of New York Press, 1972.

Gabrieli, Francesco. *Arab Historians of the Crusades.* E.J. Costello, tr. New York: Dorset Press, 1957.

Al-Hassan, Ahmad Y. and Donald R. Hill. *Islamic Technology: An Illustrated History.* Cambridge: Cambridge University Press, 1986.

John R. Hayes, ed. *The Genius of Arab Civilization: Source of Renaissance.* London: Eurabia Publications Ltd., 1983.

Ibn Mounkidh, Ousama. *The Autobiography of Ousama.* George Richard Potter, tr. New York: Harcourt Brace and Company, 1929.

Lane-Poole, Stanley. *Saladin and the Fall of the Kingdom of Jerusalem.* New York: G.P. Putnam's Sons, 1898.

Maalouf, Amin. *The Crusades Through Arab Eyes.* Jon Rothschild, tr. New York: Schocken Books, 1984.

Regan, Geoffrey. *Saladin and the Fall of Jerusalem.* London: Croom Helm, 1987.

Riley-Smith, Jonathan, ed. *The Oxford Illustrated History of the Crusades.* Oxford: Oxford University Press, 1995.

Rosebault, Charles. *Saladin: Prince of Chivalry.* New York: Robert M. McBride & Company, 1930.

Runciman, Steven. *A History of the Crusades, vol. 1-3.* Cambridge: Cambridge University Press, 1962.

Shatzmiller, Maya, ed. *Crusaders and Muslims in Twelfth-Century Syria.* Leiden: E.J. Brill, 1993.

Slaughter, Gertrude. *Saladin (1138-1193).* New York: Exposition Press, 1955.

Waddy, Charis. *Women in Muslim History.* London: Longman Press, 1980.

WEB SOURCES

http://www.fordham.edu/halsall/sbook1k.html

Internet Medieval Sourcebook–along with the Hanover College source below, this is *the* internet site for a wide variety of history resources, texts, and artwork on this and many other topics from the medieval period.

http://history.hanover.edu/medieval/crusades.html

The Crusades–primary source texts and resource links; similar to the Medieval Sourcebook, but not as extensive.

http://familiar.sph.umich.edu/cgfa/crusades/crusades.html

The Crusades: A Chronicle in Art–not very scholarly or neutral text , but this site provides good access to primary source illustrations in color.

http://w3.nai.net/~jroberts/home.htm

Early Islamic Coins–an excellent site of images of coins from the Muslim world, indexed chronologically and by ruling group.